The Big Book of Rants

A Gentleman's Bathroom Companion to
a Life in Advertising

Rich Siegel

"The very existence of flamethrowers proves that sometime, somewhere, someone said to themselves, "You know, I want to set those people over there on fire, but I'm just not close enough to get the job done."

– George Carlin

Rich Siegel is also the author of *Tuesdays With Mantu,
My Adventures with a Nigerian Con Artist ISBN 1-4134-5854-8*

*And Round Seventeen & ½, The Names Have Been Changed to
Protect the Inefficient ISBN 978-0-692-50758-2*

Rich blogs regularly at http://roundseventeen.blogspot.com

Printed in the United States of America

First Printing, 2016

ISBN:0692703314

Erupting Volcano Publications

TABLE OF CONTENTS

I

Introduction

Like many, or at least those who are 44 years old, I have a love/hate relationship with advertising.

I love that I found a way to make a living stringing one word after another and leveraging my admittedly sophomoric sense of humor.

I love that I did not get shoe-horned into the world of certified public accounting, with its capitol expenditures, complicated debits and long-term tax-deferred credits. Or some other occupational field my parents deemed solid and capable of producing a reliable income. Like the law, mechanical engineering or dentistry --though the proximity to laughing gas and the opportunity to inflict searing pain on so many of life's inconsiderate cretins is not without its charms.

I love how at no point in my life have I ever owned more than one suit. And that getting dressed for work in the morning was the same on Monday as it was on the previous Sunday. And that cargo shorts, a ratty T-shirt and some stinky flip-flops were standard business attire in a business that cared less about what you put on your body and more about the quality of work you put on the table.

I love working with smart people. And that I have had the opportunity to rub shoulders, break bread and go toe-to-toe in creative "discussions" with the industry's smartest and most talented folks, including Lee Clow, Steve Hayden, David Lubars, John Doyle and many more. I've also had the misfortune of working with some of the dumbest, witless, most incompetent human sacks of flesh to ever walk the Earth, but we'll get to that shortly.

I love how advertising has the capacity to surprise. And that ideas, once deemed too risky or unconventional, can leap frog ahead of others and with Big Bang improbability somehow spring to life.

My love affair with advertising was solidified on a hot summer morning, in August of 1997, when my partner John Shirley and I were returning to our offices on the Westside of Los Angeles after completing a voiceover recording deep in the bowels of Hollywood. On our drive home, and with no warning from the media department, we started seeing yellow billboards from our infamous ABC campaign. They were along Western Ave. They were on the Santa Monica freeway. They were on buses going up and down Lincoln Blvd. They were everywhere – an unheard of rotation of a dozen different headlines.

Not only were they visible, they were audible.

At lunchtime, we found ourselves at the Rose Café in Venice and people were talking about these yellow billboards, our yellow billboards. They were repeating the lines. And laughing. Out loud. Not LOL'ing into their keyboards or smart-phones. But laughing…out…loud.

And it wasn't just in LA. It was happening in New York, Chicago, San Francisco and Miami.

It was a magical and surreal moment in time and as my prescient partner put it, *"it's never going to get any better than this."*

And it didn't.

What advertising was and what it has become are two different animals. One, a panda bear cub you want to play with and cuddle and feed only the best free range bamboo shoots. The other, a vicious pitbull, with a taste for blood, sporting a spiked metal collar that would easily rip your skin and leave you with a raging case of tetanus.

The metaphor may be a little stretched. Suffice to say that advertising in the year 2016 is supremely hate-worthy.

Between the greed, politics, title inflation, grueling hours, obscene pay inequality, restrictions on business class flights, SuperDesks™, Assistant Planners, Associate Planners, Group Planning Directors, brand engagement units, daily check-ins, holding company shenanigans, Saturday status meetings, Sunday status meetings, useless corporate hierarchy, content strategy, and the obsession with the creation of Frivolous Fuckwadian Digital Knick Knacks™, I hardly know where to begin.

Oh wait, yes I do.

In 2009, I started writing about the demise of advertising (and other things) on my blog RoundSeventeen which has now amassed more than ½ million page views. The blog has given me a digital soapbox on which I may excise my demons. It's a lot cheaper than a therapist and I like to believe the discipline and process of maintaining the regular, daily output has somehow improved my copywriting.

That, of course, can easily be argued, mostly by junior planners and young Associate Creative Directors who occasionally see me walking the hallways of their high school....er, ad agencies and wonder, aloud…

"Who let grandpa in the building?"

From the blog, I have hand-curated, a very popular phrase these days, as in hand-curated mayonnaise, hand-curated flea repellent and hand-curated spackling compound, some of my favorite as well as – if I can be so assumptive—some of your favorite posts.

They have been tweaked, rewritten and in some cases expanded upon, so they will read more like true essays and less like caffeine-fueled extemporaneous brain dumps. Though rest assured the bitterness and jaded cynicism you've come to expect has not been diluted in any way.

On that same note, though the title suggests this book is a "guide to a life in advertising", one would be wise not to adhere, or even listen, to any of the counsel on the following pages. Like the hyperbolic campaign proclamations of one Donald J. Trump, these are merely suggestions. Bite-sized and edited for easy consumption, ideally, as the title indicates, while seated in the bathroom.

Nor was there any sexual discrimination intended by the use of the term 'Gentleman.' It just seemed more colloquial. So if you're going to write me angry letters, I'd prefer they would be about something else.

Finally, depending where you find yourself on the advertising spectrum, whether you're young or old, client or agency, management or labor, creative or planning, or simply prefer toasted bagels to untoasted bagels, it's a good bet you'll either love these rants. Or hate them.

Frankly, I hope it's a little of both.

Anger Mismanagement

Anger has gotten a bad name.

Given a choice, most employers would fire an angry employee before an incompetent employee (I know this from experience.) We suppress anger. We hide it from our kids. We walk away from anger, at least when it comes to advertising, when we should be embracing it.

Take Apple's 1984 commercial for example.

Regarded as the best commercial ever committed to celluloid, the spot hinges on anger. When viewing the first rough cut, no one said, "Does she have to be so angry?"

Without her frustration, boiled to perfection, there is no spot.

And while there is much to be learned from the greatest commercial ever made, we, the craftsmen and craftswomen of today's advertising, are determined to take nothing from it.

Nothing.

Because the moment a client catches the slightest whiff of anger in a script, or a performance, or even in the enthusiastic defense of an idea, the review instinct kicks in and the call to a new agency consultant is made.

That's how averse we have become to anger.

As a result we are left with an endless stream of formulaic commercials in every variety of mind-numbing cheeriness:

Bite and Smile

Drive and Smile

Wipe and Smile

Get a Free Credit Report and Smile

Furnish a Living Room and Smile

Get Unlimited Text & Data and Smile

and of course,

Conquer Erectile Dysfunction Sit in a Clawfoot Tub and Smile.

But the truth is, happiness is cheap. It's boring. And does nothing to spark my interest.

Whereas anger is real. Authentic. And when left in its purest undistilled form, the most entertaining.

When I turn to Yelp or Glassdoor or any of the consumer generated review sites, the one star reviews are so much more compelling and informative than the 5 star reviews. I could spend an entire morning in bed, cozied up with a warm blanket and nonstop stream of well-worded, steaming disgruntled employee invective.

If clients were smart they'd tap into this largely untapped emotion and beat their competitors to the punch with spots that are brimming with rage.

But my experience tells me clients, and many creative directors, are not smart and will always default to the pre-digested bite size nuggets of non-confrontational conformity.

And that has always, and will continue to, make me angry.

How Big Can We Get?

I started my copywriting career at the now defunct Abert, Newhoff & Burr, but things didn't really click until I moved over to Chiat/Day (the proper name for the agency, BTW.) There, I had the pleasure of working in the vicinity of the Grouchy One, Jay Chiat.

Every new employee was given a little red handbook, entitled: *Quotations from Chairman Jay.* In it, was the collected wisdom and seeming incongruencies of the man and the agency.

For instance, Jay loudly and proudly proclaimed, "I see everything that goes out the door." This was followed quickly by a directive to his executive assistant, "Why are you showing me this?"

I bring this up because the conundrum that Jay faced in 1994, still haunts us today. Only it has gotten worse.

Let's step back for a second.

There was a time when amongst the thousands of assignments floating around the agency, everyone recognized the ones that were "D&D" or simply Down and Dirty. The pay-the-bills schlock that needed to be executed, expedited and expectorated with the least amount of effort.

The back of an FSI.

The 5 second tag on a Tier Two spot.
The 10 second live radio DJ read.
The race win ad at the Des Moines BMX quarterfinals.
The 78 X 125 thumbnail banner ad for *Harvard Business Review.*

There was an unspoken understanding that, placed in the hands of competent, talented creatives, these little down and dirty jobs could be handled quickly and efficiently. That understanding was expelled from the building. Along with the fax machines and the notion that employees should have weekends off.

Today, there are no down and dirty jobs. Everything, and I mean everything, is a 5-Alarm Fire Drill. Worthy of late night Pad Thai Noodles, a few wasted weekends and a 138 page deck.

Gotta have a deck.

"If we don't get this hang tag right, those guys from Droga5 will sweep in here and steal this account."

"The new Tweet has been approved by the Group Creative Director who needs to show it to the Executive Creative Director who needs to run it by the Chief Creative Officer who will then pass it on to the CEO."

"Where are we on the 17th round of revisions to the CTA?"

Not only does my observation apply to everything, it applies to everywhere.

As I've noted before, as a freelancer I work in many, many different agencies of all shapes and sizes. And I've seen this expensive phenomena of micro-management across the board.

A few months ago I sat in on a conference call. And as the Assistant Associate Planner of Experiential Digital Strategies was merging trapezoids and parallelograms via the magic of Powerpoint, I took the time to scan through the meeting attendee list.

There were no less than 47 people on the call.

That's two football teams. Two baseball teams. And seven guys in the Men's Room standing way too close to each other at the stadium stainless steel pee trough.

Jay Chiat once famously asked, "How big can we get before we get bad?"

He might have added, "How big can we get before we get bloated?"

Regrets? I Have a Few.

I wrote hundreds of Apple ads and never listened to a word Steve Jobs had to say.

Of course an opening line like that begs for some explanation. So here goes.

In 1993 I was lured away from Chiat/Day/Los Angeles to work at BBDO on Wilshire Blvd. Though I had a head for math, science and calculus, I had no experience with computers at all. That didn't seem to bother the powers that be.

They hired me to write copy and that's what I did. Often until 1 or 2 in the morning, pending many layers of corporate approval.

You see, Steve Jobs was no longer with the company. It was being run by John Scully and his band of witless, former PepsiCo executives. These brown fizzy sugar water marketing professionals believed they could turn the Mac into America's favorite business machine.

They didn't.

I don't like staying late at the office. I like it even less dealing with brown fizzy sugar water imbeciles who can't make up their mind.

Or who make up their mind only to have that decision overturned by a brown fizzy sugar water VP on a higher rung of the corporate ladder.

I was miserable.

I left that job and ended back at home at Chiat/Day. Almost about the same time Steve Jobs ended up back home at Apple.

In 1998, the resurgence of Apple was well underway. I had some minor successes at Chiat at about the same time. It was then that Lee Clow approached me.

"Rich, one of the senior writers on Apple is going back to NY. We need a guy who can channel Steve's voice and write copy that demystifies sophisticated computers. I want to throw your oversized hat in the ring."

Lee gave me a weekend to mull over the proposition.

If I could take back that Monday morning before the turn of the century I would.

Here I was, being given an opportunity to work with one of the most influential men in the history of mankind. A chance to be part of the iPod, the iPhone and the complete democratization of technology. A ground floor, once in a lifetime bite at the Apple that could have changed the course of my career and made me and future generations of Siegels fabulously wealthy.

I said "No" when I probably should have said "Yes." Swayed perhaps by one last comment from Lee.

"I know you like to write funny. But Steve doesn't do funny."

Maybe I made the right decision after all.

Where are All the Good Ideas?

I have a good idea: let's stop saying, "a good idea can come from anyone and anywhere."

It's bullshit.
And the people spouting that nonsense know it's bullshit.

It's Morale Building 101.

"Yeah, we can't give out raises or bonuses this year. And nobody gets an office. And we'll need you to work the weekend, Christmas weekend, but the good news is we're all in this together and who knows who'll come up with the big game changing idea."

Based on years of experience, I can tell you it won't be the Assistant Account Coordinator who regularly messes up the late night dinner orders.

It won't be the old media dude who has been crunching numbers since they introduced the Donovan Data System.

And I'll put my nuts on the block and posit it won't be the bean-counting office manager Nazi who has set up a Dropcam in the mailroom to see who has been pinching the purple Post It Notes.

Because here's the truth of the matter, a good idea is rare.

And it needs to be nurtured, protected and supported.

Not tossed in the waste basket because it's only the first or second round of presentations. Not marginalized because it's a smidge to the left or right of the precious strategy. And not minimized by pinning it up on a wall with a hundred, scratch that, a thousand mediocre ideas gathered at the agency brainstorming session.

Or *Idea Rumble.*

Or *Synapse Symposium.*

Or *Conceptapolluzza.*

Or whatever *fakakta* name some clever ass-nugget in the Planning Department came up with.

I'm all for the democratization of technology, but diametrically opposed to its ugly cousin, the commoditization of creativity.

There isn't a formula for what we do. There's no science to it. It's a little commerce mixed in with a lot of magic. And sometimes the recipe can be amended with a generous serving of caffeine and a dash of Vicodin.

Moreover, it takes experience. I didn't have a good idea until I spent 17 years spitting out bad ones.

Sadly, at least in the ad world, we are not drowning in a sea of good ideas. The landscape is as barren as a 10 acre parcel of unsold land in the Mojave desert.

Of course, this is just my opinion. A perspective. A theory, if you will.

Should you require any further evidence, I invite you to turn on your television.

Why I Sucked at Being a Creative Director

Using generous math, and including the time I was an Associate Creative Director (a worthless title if there ever was one), I spent roughly 10 years as a bonafide Creative Director.

With the benefit of hindsight and a heaping helping of self-deprecation, here's why I sucked at the job:

1. **Immovable as a Dead Donkey.** Like all Siegels I have inherited a generations-long stubborn streak. It's deeply embedded within my DNA. In some instances it disguises itself as Persistence or Determination. And has served me well in running marathons or getting a movie produced or a book published. But in the case of being a Creative Director at an advertising agency, where there is a premium on building consensus, accommodating cretinous client demands and answering to faceless holding company officers, that same stubborn streak has done me a distinct disservice. Earning me the unhealthy reputation of being an ass. An immovable one at that.

2. **Art Before Commerce.** Young creatives often find mentors or role models to look up to. More often it's a matter of studying their work in the One Show Book or CA annuals and mimicking (stealing) their style. When I was learning the business, the writer I most respected was Mark Fenske. His work was always smart, always different, and always courageous. Mark subscribed to the auteur theory, that advertising should reflect a personal vision. And stand on

its own as a piece of communication worth experiencing.
I always challenged myself, and my teams, to those type
of standards. Sometimes we measured up. Most times we
didn't. But the process was never ever pretty. (see point #1)

3. **Dirty Hands.** Unlike most Creative Directors, I was never
able to walk away from the keyboard. I always kept my hand
in the making of ads. Competing with the teams that were
working for me. Was it always fair? No, but it was my
responsibility to always put the best work in front of the
client. I like to think this kind of demanding work environment made any creatives working for me, better creatives. I
do know that I fought as hard for their work as I did for any
of mine. Of course any admiration from my colleagues was
far surpassed by the contempt and scorn of those in Account
Management and Account Planning who took issue with my
pugilistic defense of the work. (again, see point #1)

4. **Terrible at Chess.** I know my way around rooks and bishops,
kings and queens. I even won some chess tournaments while
in college. But when all those moving pieces have moving
mouths, then it's no longer a game. You see being a Creative
Director is often about knowing which client is on the
ascent and which one isn't. It's about knowing how to make a
CMO look like a hero. It's about relationships with a capital
R. This was all squarely out of my comfort zone. I never had
the patience, nor the ability, to keep track of the internal
machinations within the client's marketing department. I
have a wife and two daughters, I have a hard enough time
keeping a lid on that dysfunctional dynamic. (This has little
to do with point #1, however I'm sure you can imagine

the aforementioned stubbornness never helped matters.)

5. **Bad Geography.** A long time ago I made the mistake of setting up shop on the West Coast, where sensitivities are high and the beautifully-tanned California skin is awfully thin. Take the simple phrase, "Get out of my office, asshole." Spoken to a colleague here in the homogenized, touchy-feely confines of West L.A., that off-the-cuff type utterance would often earn me an immediate trip to the Human Resources office. But in New York City, where I should have stayed, "Get off of my office, asshole", would merit a completely different response, like, "Up yours, douchebag. We still on for drinks after work?" See the difference?

6. **Replace Filter as Necessary.** Another reason I sucked at being a Creative Director is that I never mastered the art of not saying what I was thinking. If a synapse fired in the cortex, you can be sure the tongue and the lips were going to respond accordingly. Not always a good idea. However I am getting better at this. And to that end, I think I'll pay heed to that older and wiser little voice in my head that is telling me to hold off on points 7-100.

I'll save those for a rainy day.
Or better yet, I'll save them for myself.

Intellectual Capital

Good God!

Last week Google unveiled its new revamped logo. The effort was the culmination of work by Stanford-educated millennials, who majored in industrial design and minored in Organic Chemistry, Quantum Physics and International Geo-Politics. Millions of dollars worth of higher education focused like a laser on getting the angle of curvature on the lower portion of the letter 'g' just right.

"It's too swoopy. And indicates we are a soft, malleable company without a direction or strategy for the future."

"On the other hand, if the angle is too abrupt, it says we are a robotic company without a stake in humanity. Mmmmm?"

"Let's schedule a 2 A.M. loopback session with the team."

"I'll reserve the Armageddon War Room."

"I'll have my assistant order the Mushu Pork."

And that's where we are at in America.

Refreshing logos, while the Chinese figure out how to make things better, cheaper and faster. While India transcends the boundaries of time and space and talks us through all our customer service and software problems. And while Israel creates and develops the kind of advanced technology that even the most ardent BDS supporters can't wait to get their hands on.

We tweak logos.

We remove serifs.

We put out billion dollar press releases patting ourselves on the back for this remarkable advancement.

I don't say this enough, but I've been fortunate enough to make a career in advertising. Where, despite all the insanity, I have worked with some of the smartest, funniest, most creative people on the planet.

I've seen people tackle the most complex marketing problems and author solutions that are nothing less than remarkable in their beauty, simplicity and "Damn-I-wish-I-would-have-thought-of-that"-ness.

Of course, nine times out of ten, those solutions were met by a stone-faced client…

"What else have you got?"

I've seen resilience. Talented writers, artists, and thinkers, sent back to the drawing board over and over again. And delivering answers, again and again and again. Some better than the first. Others, not so much.

And I've seen dogged determination. There's a kid who works at an agency where I often put in some time. He must be a cyborg. No one works harder. Or longer. He has a better work ethic than 535 members of Congress.

Combined.

It all has me scratching my head, wondering how have we managed to waste so much good intellectual capitol on banner ads, digital gadgets and TV commercials that have a shelf life of a terminally-ill housefly?

Maybe I'll do some research on the topic.

Bet I can find the answer over on Google.

The Two Faces of Advertising

If you're looking for hypocrisy in advertising you don't have to look very far.

Last week, Crispin Porter & Bogusky, arguably one of the most creative shops in the land, fired their CEO and Chief Creative Officer Andrew Keller, one of the most talented creative guys in the land.

This, after 17 years of service.

17 years that produced Subservient Chicken, Whopper Freakout and a Mini campaign that set the bar for automotive advertising.

I don't know Mr. Keller and obviously have no agenda sucking up to a guy who is no longer employed, but 17 years is a long time, enough time to raise a child and send her a thousand miles away to pay outrageous, out of state college tuition.

Call me crazy, but whatever happened to this thing we call loyalty?

Every day I hear or read about the demise of agency/client relationships. Or the importance of establishing an AOR. Or how long term strategic marketing problems cannot be solved by short term, flighty jump ball assignments. But you plunk a microphone in front of an ad agency CEO and you're going to get a bloviating earful about loyalty.

We talk passionately about it and then we cavalierly axe people who have steadily drank the Kool Aid and bled the agency's team colors. I personally know of other ad folk, with a dozen, twenty and close to thirty years of service, tossed to the curb like some inedible, stale bear claw.

It doesn't end there.
Hardly.

Agencies are fond of getting on a soapbox and informing the world that "we are storytellers and artists." They talk a big game about how creative departments need to include poets, architects, musicians, photographers and not just people focused on advertising. And then they chain those people to their desks, or a long picnic table, and carve 80 hours a week out of their lives to do nothing but advertising.

Agencies can never stop talking about the power of social media. But when was the last time you read an agency blog or engaged with an agency website or sat through an entire agency self promo? I'd prefer to be drawn and quartered, at least my back would get a good stretch.

Agencies like to position themselves as leading pop culture. Of being on the cutting edge, a model of progressive thinking. And yet if you were to break down the demographics of the leadership, you'd have a hard time finding any women. Or African Americans. Or anybody frankly, that wasn't young, white, and bearded, with a closet full of fashionable European scarves and a medicine cabinet brimming with hair product.

Don't get me wrong, I love working at an ad agency. Or at least what an ad agency used to be.

But today I enjoy it from the perspective of an outsider looking in and not the other way around.

Should Mr. Keller follow the same freelance path, and once he accepts the fact that there are no free bagels in life, I suspect that in a very short while, he will feel the same way, too.

Sweet Sweat Equity

Creative people in ad agencies want something to show for their work. They want to be able to hold it, touch it, see it and show it to other people and say, "Look what I've done."

Or, more accurately, "look what we, with the help of our client partners, a production company, a mixing house and a staff of editors and color-correction button-pushers, have done."

The point is, we want something tangible.
Something that validates our chosen line of pursuit.

Ad agencies on the other hand want, or more accurately, *need* satisfied clients. They need to keep the lights on, the bills paid and the coffee machines fully stocked. The best way to accomplish that is to fill the roster of happy clients, with more happy clients. Hopefully, with bigger budgets.

This relentless push for growth often requires time. More time than the regularly allotted 40 hours enjoyed by the average American salaried man or woman.

And so, creative people and occasionally planners who might need to redraw some Venn diagrams, are asked (maybe asked is not the right word) to sacrifice their nights and weekends. It's an ugly push-pull situation that makes for a lot of sulky dissatisfaction as well as some excellent colorful reading on glassdoor.com

Is there a solution?

I'm just a freelance copywriter with a plateful of assignments I'm putting off, but allow me to extemporize a little.

I know margins are low. And after paying out all the Chief Anthropology Officers, Experiential Ninjas and Global World International Poobah who do such heavy lifting for the holding companies, it's harder than ever for an ad agency to turn a profit.

But what about Sweat Equity?

What if for instance, for every stolen weekend, an art director or a copywriter would earn a credit. Partial credits would also be doled out for late nights. Or missed vacation time. At the end of a year, a hardworking ad agency creative could accrue a significant amount of credits.

How would those credits be paid, you might ask?

Good question.

Well, here's the thing. Ad agencies love to beat their chest about how they are a center for creativity. It's why we hear such delusional terminology as, "we're not an ad agency, we're an Idea Factory."

Or, "We incubate the imagination."

Or, "We're redefining pop culture with our unique brand of entertainvertising™."

In short, there's a lot of lip service about making stuff without ever doing anything to encourage the making of stuff. Nor giving the employees the actual time it takes to make said stuff.

So what if agencies reimbursed those credits with supplies, equipment or access to facilities that would bring the unmanifested passion of creatives to fruition? What if the credits, earned by sacrificing precious time, could be used to make a short film? Or stage an art show? Or defray the cost of self-publishing a book?

What if, and I'm just spitballing here, agencies stole a page from the early playbook of the Vatican and became the curator/sponsor of their own in-house artists? They could actually be the studio they boast so freely about in the agency credentials page. Given enough thought I think you will agree this could be a win-win situation.

I know there will be some, ok many, who will scoff and write this off as the ramblings of a naive misanthrope who is completely clueless as to the finances and operations of a modern day advertising agency.

However, I am privy to the soaring frustration and disillusionment of the creative community and I see the millions of dollars being thrown at retaining current employees and the recruitment of new ones. Millions of dollars. None of it producing any effective results.

So who's being naive?

The 33 Cushiest Jobs in Advertising

Every year Business Insider puts out a list of the 37 Wealthiest People in Advertising.

Some years, it's 35.
Others, it's 38.

The number doesn't matter, the obscene truckloads of cash is what matters.

Lately, I've noticed some PR-leery big wigs are shying away from the list and choosing not to lay their cocks on the table for all the world to see. Maybe it occurred to these tone-deaf fat cats that some Assistant Account Executive who hasn't had a raise or seen a Christmas bonus in seven years might be reading about their piggish salaries and stock options, and start asking questions.

I know I have questions.

I've been in this business for 30 years. But Rich, you're 44 years old, did you skip 10th grade and go directly into copywriting? Let's not get bogged down by arithmetic and the gyrations of the sun and Earth.

The point is, I know how an ad agency works.

There are many moving parts. The Creative Department, the Account Management Department, the Broadcast

Production Department, the Operations people and of course, the always expanding, always shape-shifting Media Department.

I also have a general idea of how the departments interact with each other to gestate campaigns, bring them to the unsuspecting public and steward a brand towards mediocrity.

What I don't understand are the people who have escaped the daily grind, who no longer deal with the day-to-day insanity and haven't sat in a status meeting since 1998. These are the people on the Business Insider List. They have long titles that usually include one or more of the following words:

Global
Regional
Experiential
Innovation
International

I know how much money they're making in terms of salary, stock options and various "performance" - based bonuses.

I know where they sit on the plane, regardless if the flight is less than 6 hours and does not cross international borders.

Thanks to ample photo-posting on social media, I know their yachts.
Their favorite rosé wine.
And the opulent hotels they stay at while in Cannes.

I also know these are not the people fielding phone calls
from angry clients because the car in the commercial was Jet
Black and not Onyx Black.

Or lugging foam core boards to the 7 AM pitch in Cincinatti
for the prestigious Southern Ohio Hardee's Franchisees.

Or sitting in on a focus group, eating wet tuna fish sandwiches while watching a group of over-animated Houston
housewives decimate six, long, hard fought, weekend-less
months of creative development.

I know so much about these folks.

What I don't know and what I'd still like to know is…

…what the fuck do these people *do*?

We Can't Afford the Big Boy.

Staying busy as a freelance copywriter is a matter of lining up the next gig before the current gig is over. To that end, I am often trolling the internet, scouring job boards, making note of account changes and sniffing out turmoil.

Turmoil, as I often tell others, is a freelancer's best friend.

"Oh, the ECD got quit?"

That means there's a power vacuum. And nervous account people – like space – abhor a vacuum. They want their clients in the hands of seasoned and even sometimes cynical veterans. I know it's hard to believe there's cynicism out there, but if you look hard, you'll find it.

Recently I found an interesting job listing.

An agency in town was looking for a Freelance Jr. Copywriter. They specifically requested a junior and not a middleweight or even a senior.

By the way, just for fun I applied for the job. It only required one click of the mouse and I like to picture the recruiter scratching her head thinking, "Isn't 44 a little old for a Junior Copywriter?"

Then it occurred to me that this one little job listing was the perfect microcosm of our industry and its current state of demise.

You see when an agency says they are looking for a junior copywriter, they are looking for someone cheap. Cheap, as in we don't want to spend the extra few hundred dollars it might cost to bring in a middleweight, we'd rather trust the brand viability of our clients to someone who still doesn't know the difference between your and you're.

Someone who writes by day and experiments with hipster hairstyles by night.

Someone who has never heard of Jay Chiat and thinks Lee Clow is an appetizer at a Dim Sum Bar.

Hiring a junior freelance copywriter is also incredibly nearsighted. Oh sure you might save dollars in the short term, but with all the rewrites, the do-overs and the supervisory hours wasted in mentoring, those savings vanish quite quickly.

It's like those mathematically-impaired people who visit seedy strip mall shops to borrow money against their pay-check and get sucked into a vortex of spiraling interest costs. They leave those places with fleeting satisfaction and just enough money in their pocket to go next door for two chocolate donuts. Or as they refer to it – dinner.

It's all part of the commoditization of advertising. Where ideas and creativity have taken a backseat to SuperDesks™ and low-cost Army Grade toilet paper in the bathrooms.

Which makes this a great time to remind ourselves of the Golden Rule of Commerce:

You get what you pay for.

Followed by the second Golden Rule:

Rich Siegel.
Three writers for the price of two.™

Who's in the Mood for Tail?

Last week it was announced that Darden, the operator of many family restaurant chains like Olive Garden and Longhorn Steakhouse, was putting the Red Lobster account up for review. Sales had been falling, franchisee's were getting unhappy and the advertising had gotten stale.

Cue the eager agency contenders.

I know from experience, weekends will be sacrificed in the pursuit of this crown jewel of advertising. People will work long hours. Couches will get slept on. Cold coffee will get nuked. And strategies will be constructed, deconstructed and put before the knowing eye of focus groups.

Backs will get stabbed. Inter-office jockeying will occur. And new office romances will bloom, fed by the aphrodisiacal aromas of stale pizza and 11 PM body odor.

At the end of the review process, an agency will be selected, champagne will be uncorked and a brand-spanking new Red Lobster campaign will be foisted on the crustacean-hungry masses...

"TAIL"
:30

Open on hot melted butter drizzled over freshly steamed lobster tail.

Cut to tight shot of tongs placing lobster tail on a beautifully-dressed dinner plate.

Cut to steam rising off the fluffy mashed potatoes.

Cut to dinner roll being cracked in half.

Cut to extreme slow motion shot of flakes flying off the dinner roll.

Cut to beet red lobster tail shell being cracked open.

Cut to man wearing khaki pants, with extremely white teeth, biting into said lobster and smiling.

Cut to khaki pants man's wife, she is smiling too.

ANNCR: Right now during Red Lobster Red Tag Dining Days, you can get our signature lobster tail, mashed potatoes and your choice of farm fresh vegetable for only $9.99. Come on in now, we'll start melting the butter just for you.

End on beauty shot of dinner plate.

Starburst: Red Tag Dining Days. Just $9.99

Art Card: Red Lobster. Who's in the Mood for Tail?

I Don't Get Planning.

I won't beat around the bush.

When it comes to ad agency planning, I just don't get it.
Newsflash, I don't ever plan to get it.

I don't want to offend anyone, but in the twenty five plus
years – oh shit, now it's thirty plus years – I've been in the
business I have never depended on the planning department,
and whatever it is they do, to inch me any closer to a creative
solution.

Not once.

Ever.

Never.

And I have been forced to sit through thousands of planning
department briefings.

In the automotive world, I've heard the word "luxury"
dissected 18 ways 'til Sunday.

In the technology world, "innovation" has been picked over
like a dead water buffalo under the Serengeti sun.

Once, while pitching Sparklett's water, our MBA-enhanced
planner with the grating British accent graced us with his

business acumen and told us the strategy was all about "Blue."

By the way, Blue was the result of a two month-long 'deep dive' and a five-city tour of focus groups that I believe included a trip to the planner's home town of West Kensington.

Years ago I was at an unnamed ad agency eavesdropping – thank you open office plan – on a group of unnamed account planners and unnamed account executives talking about a unnamed brand of tortilla chips.

Personally, I don't see how a briefing about a low-interest tortilla chip could merit a meeting lasting more than 3 minutes, but this one went on longer than the *Wolf of the Wall Street*.

The ensuing question/answer/further discussion period was like an aural root canal.

"People like sharing tortilla chips."

"The spots should be about Tortilla Chip Moments."

"We need a tortilla chip manifesto."

Hear that? That's the sound of creative people rethinking their career choice.

And yet the insanity continues.

As you are reading this rather-restrained rant, there are conference rooms chock full of creatives who have just presented their ideas to a bunch of over-critical, over-thinking planners, who are over-zealously picking it apart and measuring the work against some insipid set-in-stone briefing document.

As sure as the mustache under my nose, some 26-year old ex-sorority girl with a certificate in planning and two years of real world living, is chiming in with the ubiquitous:

"I like it. And I don't want to split hairs, maybe it's in the semantics, but (and here comes the phrase that kills all good ideas) *I'm not sure it's on-strategy."*

To which, just once, I wish one ballsy staff creative would simply rise to the occasion, stand up and reply:

"Maybe, the strategy is off-strategy."

Today's Dirty Word: Collaboration.

This will come as no surprise, but I'm an old school guy. I'm not sure when that transition happened, but it did. And as my buddy recently told me, it's best to just own it.

So I do, confident that my first hand memories of printed polyester shirts and the Watergate hearings have nothing to do with my ability to out-think, out-write and out-perform today's crop of copywriters.

However, I cannot hide my disdain for this new term that is creeping into agency life wherever I go.

I'm talking about *collaboration*.

It's the notion that if two people, an art director and a copywriter, are good at coming up with creative solutions to a challenge, then four people, or six people, or eight people, are even better.

I'm familiar with this approach when it comes to codeine-enhanced cough medicine. And can attest to its euphoric efficacy. Three teaspoons of Promethazine are always better than one.

But it doesn't work that way when it comes to work.

Collaboration simply muddies the water. Even the term bothers me. I can't help think of the Vichy government who collaborated with, and were puppets of, the Nazi regime.

I can't imagine how young people today, who may be drinking the collaboration Kool Aid, can stand out and make a name for themselves and their work if they are content to throw all their ideas into the collective bucket of mediocre groupthink.

You see, when I find myself briefed with other teams on a big project, I don't want to work with them. I want my partner and I to beat the pants off them. I want our ideas to outshine theirs. So that when the next big project comes along the powers that be say, *"let's get that angry old fat dude and his partner, they had some killer ideas."*

I'll take competition over collaboration any day of the week.

I still have a vivid, photographic memory of a weekend spent at the old Chiat/Day warehouse. We were in the throes of a 100 million dollar pitch. We gathered in The Fish, a Gehry-designed conference room shaped like the inside of a sperm whale, and presented work to Clow and Kuperman.

My partner and I were guppies swimming with sharks. The rock stars of the business: Rabosky, Butler, Feakens, Gentile, Siltanen, Rice, Sweitzer, Hooper, Vincent, Jordan, Curtis, Hughes, Dunkle, et al.

Each team stood up and, hoping not to embarrass themselves, and presented their best thinking. The tension was high. But the desire to best the other teams was even higher.

And guess what? It worked.

Everyone, through the process of competitive humiliation, got better. Not unlike hot steel being forged into a precision sushi knife.

There was a time when I knew all the names of all the people in the ad business who were doing the good work. Now, thanks to collaboration and the demise of the star system, I don't know any.

Or, maybe I do know their names but can't remember them.

Hell, I can't remember where I left my reading glasses.

Not Messing with Texas.

Many of my friends and colleagues are visiting the Lone Star State.

I am not.

In fact, I've only stepped foot in Texas once. San Antonio, to be more specific. For 5 minutes. Possibly the happiest 5 minutes of my life.

You see, three hours earlier my partner and I had stepped onto a miniature Lear Jet in Van Nuys, CA. It was the first time I'd ever flown in a private jet so I was unfamiliar with the accommodations. As we neared our cruising altitude of 47,000 feet I felt the urge to relieve myself. The flight attendant/co-pilot/baggage handler told me I was more than welcome to use the facility.

In order to do my business I would have to get on my knees and crawl into a tiny space outfitted with an even tinier port-a-potty. All next to a paper-thin wall separating me from my boss.

It was a no-go, no-flow zone as far as I was concerned. Fortunately, we had to touch down in San Antonio to refuel the jet in order to reach our destination, Tampa Bay.

As soon as the ground crew guy unlatched the door I bolted out like an angry bull in a rodeo pen.

I have different memories for different cities. San Antonio will always be about removing the spur in my bladder.

That is not to tar the entire state of Texas.

In fact, I wouldn't mind seeing Austin.

I hear it's pretty cool. Or as the kids like to say "sic" or "tight" or "dope." By the way, if you're over 35 years in age, and I am so this applies to me as well, you should never utter the phrase, "that's dope."

If I ever do make it to Austin it most certainly won't be for the SXSW.

As many of you know, I abhor large crowds.

I especially abhor large crowds of affected advertising people. And finally I have no tolerance for large crowds of affected advertising people sporting knit caps, dreads and friendship bracelets, pontificating about what we can all look forward to in the years ahead.

Pontification and unfounded opinionating should be conducted by bald, cynical industry veterans, alone in their den, with ample caffeine, Vicodin and fading memories of glorious days gone past.

That said, if you are in Austin for the SXSW, here are my top five can't miss panels and discussion groups you won't want to skip:

Media Planning Forum to Synthesize Transparent Infrastructures, Tuesday 9:30 AM at the Digital Palapa

Chief Innovation Officers Panel on the Future Incubation of B2B Paradigms, Wednesday 11:30 AM at the Westin Kale Bar and Juicing Station

Productizing Dynamic Channels and Best Practice Web Services, Wednesday 1:30 PM in the Pop-Up Parking Lot

Recontextualizing the Scalable Workspace Via The Community Table and Particle Board Extension Leafs, Thursday 6:30 AM, hosted by the Barbarian Group

Maximizing Upward Profit Distribution to the C-Suite Through Fear, Merciless Attrition and Next Generation Accounting Principles, Friday 10:00 AM at the Ponzi Room and again Saturday 8:30 PM in the Carlo Gambino Conference Center

The Lost Art of Underthinking.

I was in a meeting about a month ago. Actually, it does me no good to pinpoint the date of this meeting because I was in the same meeting 2 months ago. Two years ago. 5 years ago. And 10 years ago.

You know the meeting.

A dozen of the agency's top minds gathered to share their opinions, ply their office politics and grandstand on a do-little, utterly-disposable, completely-mindless piece of crap communication that will cost $581,327 in research, labor and man hours to produce. And return $27 in actual revenue.

I'm no Nobel-Prize winning economist Milton Friedman – we had the Friedmans over for Passover once and Roy Friedman drank all the Slivovitz and started dancing with the drapes – but that's got nothing to do with the topic at hand.

Is it any wonder why ad agencies can't make any money these days and demand employees put in 80 hour weeks while chained to the SuperDesk™.

The simplest down-and-dirty, get-it-out-the-door project has become a mental clusterfuck that makes the current Sunni/Shia/ISIS/Yazedi crisis look like child's play.

And media fragmentation has only exacerbated the situation.

It may take a village to raise a child, but it takes a battalion to put together a banner ad. A small army to spit out an FSI. And a full-blown coalition to concept a simple TV spot.

Not since the last congressional caucus have I seen so many people accomplishing so little.

And yet the good folks in HR are still hiring more.

We don't need more.
We need less.

In fact we need less of everything.
Less people in the room.
Less input.
Less data.
Less client feedback.
Less testing.
Less tweaking.
Less pages in the deck.
Less Powerpoints.
Less layers.
Less top management.
Less circle backs, deep dives and base touching.
Less devil's advocates.

We need to do more with our gut.
Less with our brain.

And in the spirit of celebrating less, I will say no more.

My Plans to be a Planner

Stop me if you've seen this movie before.

And I wouldn't be surprised if you had, because this scenario plays out every day in every ad agency across the country, from the wickedly-inspired hallways of Wieden & Kennedy in Portland to the anabolic steroid-laced hallways of Zimmerman Advertising in Fort Lauderdale.

A senior planner hands a Creative Director a meticulously-crafted planning brief.

He or she is peacock proud of the brief's brevity, insight and searing understanding of the human condition. As the sacred document is passed from one professional to the next, a slight addendum is added.

"We need to show the client something in three days."

"Slow your roll," the Creative Director responds, "How long have you been working on this brief?"

"About two months. We had initial research. Data Analysis. Loop backs. Deep dives. More research. Oh and then the CMO went to Machu Pichu. So really only 6 weeks," the planner replies, with not a hint of guilt.

The Creative Director, having just enrolled her kids in an expensive private school, bites her lip and tells her team to do the best they can.

And in three days time they do.

The work goes down to the client and in one of those meetings that can only happen in advertising, the Associate Chief Marketing Officer claims he never signed off on the initial brief.

He seizes the opportunity to do a little grandstanding of his own, because he just put a down payment on a Porsche Carerra, and instructs the agency to come back with work in a different direction.

His direction.

The senior planner, with all the various degrees in demographics, psychographics and social media metric confabulation, could push back and contest the point, but he and his wife just bought a new town home. And the formica counters in the kitchen need to be replaced with granite.

And so, the original precious planning brief, the one that incubated for 6 weeks and was slaved over with loving care and undue attention, is tossed in the trash can in favor of a new brief. The one that was angrily ad-libbed by the ambitious Associate CMO who is itching to get in his Porsche and tell the world he has a small penis.

The cynical among you, that's almost all of you, might be thinking, why do we need planning at all if the client is

going to reject our guidance and write their own briefs
based on nothing more than gut instinct and that morning's
caffeine intake?

But as a seasoned ad veteran who has spent considerable
time in the industry, I know that every problem is also an
opportunity.

The silver lining in this case is I can extend my already
lengthy career even longer by transitioning into the planning
department.

That's right, I'll become a Copywriter/Planner.

As a hybrid creative/strategist I'll be uniquely positioned to
take advantage of the aforementioned scenario. And short
circuit the all-too-familiar strategic clusterfuck to my
advantage.

For instance, I don't need 6 weeks to write a crappy brief. I
can do it in three. Which leaves me ample time to work on
my online chess game and perfect the Sicilian Gambit.

And crappy ads for my crappy brief?
Well, God knows I have plenty of practice writing those.

It's the perfect plan for a 44 year old.

Who knows, I might get another dozen years out of this
industry.

Names Will Be Named.

Once, I made the mistake of putting a friend's name in a blog posting hoping he would understand the tongue-in-cheek nature of the piece. It backfired. I publicly apologized. And swore never to name names in any RoundSeventeen blog posting.

Today I'm welching on that promise.

For two reasons.

First, I'm getting to a privileged point in my career where I just don't give a shit anymore.

And second, I've come to the painful conclusion that what I write matters to no one because frankly no one (apart from you faithful fourteen followers) is reading what I'm writing.

So what bullshit am I calling bullshit on?

Years ago, I was in charge of advertising for El Pollo Loco advertising. They had a minuscule budget and an ambitious media plan. Somehow we had figured a way to make 45 TV commercials on less than $250,000. Even by 2004 standards, that was quite a feat.

One day, the account people requested my attendance for a meeting with the folks from Cruz Kravetz, their Hispanic marketing agency. They were going to produce some

El Pollo Loco commercials and thought it would be a good idea to get some guidance.

Wait, what?

The money I was told I didn't have for production was being used to fund the production of other commercials. Why, I naively thought, are we making two different sets of commercials?

Because, as the bullshit machine was slowly being cranked to 11, Hispanics eat El Pollo Loco's citrus-marinated, fire grilled chicken for completely different reasons than general market caucasians or African Americans.

You see, I was under the mistaken impression that people from Mexico or El Salvador or Belize might enjoy EPL because they were hungry or appreciated fresh chicken or authentic salsa and tortillas.

But that, it turns out, is a narrow white man's view of the world devoid of any ethnographic insight.

As the Cruz Kravetz experts expertly pointed out, Hispanic people are all about, "family, passion and the family-oriented, passionate preparation of food products."

And then I was treated to a cavalcade of storyboards featuring large families. Being passionate. Eating chicken. And then, impossibly, being more passionate.

If it weren't so politically incorrect I would have told these professionals exactly what I thought of their *fiesta de mierda*.

They are by no means alone in their hoodwinking.

I've never had the pleasure of sitting in with an African-American specialty boutique, but I can spot their spots a mile away. Most often in car commercials. The copy, accompanied by needle-drop 'urban' music, invariably includes nonsense like "flow", "smooth" or "get your drive on."

Frankly, if I were Hispanic or black I would be seriously offended by these clichéd marketing approaches.

Then again, who am I to judge? I'm not a member of any minority. I'm just a white Jew. And the only advertising I respond to usually involves liquidation sales or 30% discounts.

Wait a minute…

Just Say No.

As I write this it is 10 AM. I woke up an hour ago. Put on a pot of coffee. Had some low calorie cereal. Replaced the batteries on my thermostat. And played a few games of online Scrabble.

In other words, I'm not at work.

This is unusual for me, even as a freelancer. You see, this has been one incredibly busy year. I haven't worked at a lot of different agencies, but the ones I have did work for, just kept extending me.

It wasn't because they like to have some male eye candy walking the halls. They extended me because I help put out fires.

Many, many fires.

You see, I write. Whereas most of the folks who call themselves copywriters these days do not actually live up to their job title. I've seen what they do. They make presentations on Post It Notes. They conjure up InstaGrams. They mumble on about social media projects that will only be seen by 327 people.

They do everything but write.

And for me, that's the best part of ad life. I'm not big on

meetings. Or exchanging small talk in the hallways. Or "collaborating" with client partners. Particularly the latter. Because that's when what I've written gets dumbed down and becomes what a committee has unwritten.

It's when the compromises start. And never seem to end.

And if you haven't guessed, capitulating, checking off boxes, settling for mediocrity, these are not my strong suits. Once in the name of ambition, I had a stomach for it. Not anymore.

Right now I've got two, possibly three commercials, that have been approved at competing agencies. Neither of these agencies bothered to keep me on for production. I understand. Why pay me a full day rate to sit around to eat sushi and approve wardrobe selections?

Some creatives would grumble about not seeing their work through to the end. I call these people, young.

You see, the second a commercial goes into production, the client Hollywood wannabes come out of their cubicles. Suddenly everybody has an opinion.

"I don't like that actress. She reminds me of my neighbor."

"Let's shoot the red car. Or maybe the black one. The silver is nice."

"What lens is he using?"

Worst of all, when you're on a set, the tenuous power balance between agency and client is tilted in the favor of the party writing the checks.

On one unforgettable occasion and under the threat of an impending thunderstorm, a client, who had graduated with an MBA just 8 months prior to the shoot, caused a two hour delay to a tight shooting schedule, in order to angle a Jaguar XK 3 inches to the left.

THREE FUCKING INCHES!

For a shot that lasted less than 2 seconds on screen.

I'm sure he's now the CMO of a major auto manufacturer.

This was more than 10 years ago, and I'm just now purging it from my system.

So here's my compromise.

I'll write your commercials. Or your manifestos. Or your print ads. Or your radio spots. But when it comes to producing them and watching them die a thousand bureaucratic deaths, I'd prefer to stay home and eat my supermarket sushi.

It's Funny Cause Its True.

Every time I walk into a new agency, and lately that's been happening a lot, I am jumped by the HR people who insist I sign a 10 page NDA, before I step foot in the building.

In this Non-Disclosure Agreement, I agree not to disclose any pertinent information regarding the agency or, more importantly, the client I will be working on. This ominous legal agreement is meant to stem the tide of corporate espionage.

Only after I have signed the document am I allowed to discuss the latest project, often code-named like Eagle Wing or Red Box or Area 52, or some other nonsense proposed by a junior account person, in lieu of any meaningful contribution.

And only after the papers have been properly filed am I to be given a briefing of any kind.

I make my rounds in Southern California, the automotive capitol of the world.

And so, I am often called in to work on car assignments, luxury cars, SUV's, performance sedans, economy vehicles, you name it.

Today I was handed a brief for a new car, a car the account team, the planners and the client, want to portray as "innovative", "youthful" and a leader in its own "category."

That is certainly information I will hold close to the vest.

However, I hate to break it to these folks, three weeks ago I was at a different ad agency, working on a different car, and their double secret probation brief was along the lines of "innovative, youthful and industry leadership."

And next week I'm headed to another agency.

Mmmmm, I wonder what that brief will say?

In other words, it's all the same.

About the only thing that differentiates one ad agency from another, is the zip code. And the brand of cheap, sandpaper-like toilet paper found in the Men's Room.

I remember a conversation I had with a very wise account executive – that might qualify as an oxymoron. I had just spent two years working as a staffer at the agency and had been offered a promotion and a better sounding job at another agency, ironically enough in the same office building.

The executive, with many years in the agency world, cautioned me about getting my hopes too high with regards to life at the new shop.

The phrase he uttered, and a phrase I have consequently repeated to new up-and-coming writers transitioning to new jobs:

"Same shit, different shithouse."

Analog Retentive

I miss the one off.

The One Off was a singular great idea/great execution/great ad that stood alone in the limelight. It was unencumbered by contrived brand extensions. Unfettered by social media integration. And unburdened by the false prophecy of 360 degree synergy.

Look through the awards annuals of days gone by and you'll find page after page of great One Offs.

But the One Off is on the endangered species list. Today, creative directors will trash an idea simply because it is a One Off. As if that were some kind of pejorative.

Or worse, like some crazed Joe Pesci character, they'll stick a great idea in a table vice and squeeze it until it yields banners, mobile apps and "something fun we can do on Instagram."

It's all such nonsense. Sometimes a great spot is just a great spot. And that should be more than enough.

Ask the man, the woman, or the CMO on the street which brand does the best job marketing itself and you will no doubt hear, Apple. This is more than a little ironic since Apple is a company that defines the cutting edge of digital technology. Yet they refuse to play in the digital marketing arena.

When it comes to advertising they don't subscribe to the flavor of the day. They are iconoclasts. And refreshingly old school.

Steve Jobs, and his successor Tim Cook, never bought into the Java-scripted, HTML, inflective paradigm shifting mumbo jumbo that is being peddled in executive boardrooms across America.

They know snake oil when they smell it.

But what if the greatest One Off of all time, Apple's *"1984"* spot, were in the hands of folks who didn't know how to leave well enough alone?

I suspect Tank Top Girl would have her own Facebook page. We'd know where she buys her athletic shorts. The workout routine that produced such stunning triceps. And the high protein, gluten free cereal she eats every morning before her daily assault on convention.

Similarly, the Big Brother character would have his own Twitter feed. And a team of 20-something social media writers working night and day, wearing out the dictionary and the thesaurus to come up with authentic sounding Orwellian doublespeak.

And of course there would be a website where users could enter their own target of disdain and, through the magic of algorithms and UX design, see their ex-bosses, old girlfriends, and former landlords, destroyed by a rebellious airborne sledgehammer of destruction.

Oh the hours of meaningful brand engagement that would produce.

Yeah, right.

Thankfully, *1984* was not like 2016.

The Way Advertising Should Be.

If you know me, you know I do a lot of kvetching about advertising. The business is filled with so much nonsense, so much stupidity, and so many incompetent clueless people, that for an angry writer like myself, it's like shooting fish in a barrel.

And I'm talking about flat fish like halibut or flounder, that swim on their sides, so it's even harder to miss.

But today I'd like to tell a story of a different kind.

In 1994, after an incredibly frustrating year at BBDO, I was hired to work at Team One Advertising. A creative hot shop at the time, teeming with a staff of talented writers and art directors, many of whom have gone on to become the Grand Creative Poobah at places like Chiat, Dailey, RPA, McCann Erikson and such.

I had just settled into my new office, notice I didn't say cubicle, this was a time when management respected the creative process and doled out offices, with real doors and windows.

The creative director called and said one of the writers was going on vacation, back to Wisconsin for a week. He asked if I would fill in for him and work with the art director on a new beer account, Castlemaine XXXX, an Australian brew with new distribution in the US.

Naturally, I said yes. Because the boss had asked me to. Not because I had snaked the assignment away from anybody. Which has been known to happen.

The XXXX people wanted to position their suds as the authentic beer of the Australian Outback. And they wanted to use outdoor boards, my favorite media. So the art director and I cranked up the headline machine and started spitting out funny lines.

It wasn't difficult at all. And within three days, we had enough material to cover a wall.

Here's where it gets interesting.

By Wednesday the creative director had seen all the work and culled it in half.

By Thursday we had a meeting with three of the top clients. No planner intervention. No junior clients. No focus groups. No hierarchy of any kind.

By Friday, we had approval on the campaign. Not a qualified approval. Not a pending approval. Not a let-me-show-this-to-my-wife-and-make-sure-she's-good-with-it approval.

I'm talking about a signed estimate, cash on the table, let's-do-this approval.

By the following Monday, the day the vacationing writer returned to the agency, mechanicals were already being made.

A year later, the art director and I were at Lincoln Center in NY accepting a couple of One Show Silver Pencils for the campaign that went from start to finish in less than a week.

If memory serves, we smoked fancy cigars and bought a bottle of champagne one only buys when spending someone else's money.

Thank you Saatchi & Saatchi shareholders.

Even as I write this I can't believe the surprising turn of events and the uncomplicated way the planets fell into alignment. Mostly because in the 22 years since, and the countless tales I've heard from other creatives, it's never happened that way ever again.

Ever.

Do the Rice Thing.

Years ago I was hired by the ad agency that handled the
Uncle Ben's rice account. The client, and the agency, wanted
to do a campaign that used Uncle Ben as a spokesperson.

Not a bad idea since Uncle Ben had automatic branding and
his name has been around for more than 50 years.

But it was an opportunity not without its own challenges.
There was the issue of race. This is never a minor issue, nor
should it be.

First, a little brand primer.

Back in 1947, not a great time in race relations at all, a
group of ad executives from Leo Burnett thought it would
be a good idea to give the Uncle Ben's brand a face. This
was the Leo Burnett formula. They had also given birth
to the Jolly Green Giant, Tony the Tiger and the Pillsbury
Doughboy to name a few.

They asked Frank, a maître d', an African-American maître
d', at a Chicago restaurant if he'd like to be photographed
for $500 and one day's worth of shooting. Frank agreed.
And Uncle Ben, with all its negative connotations, was
born.

Fast forward to 2007.

We, the ad agency, suggested that since the character was

strictly fictional we could take liberty and make Uncle Ben the fictional CEO of the company. Not unlike the way Jack was made the CEO of Jack in the Box.

By putting him in a high executive position we would take some of the onus off the obvious missteps of 1947. The real Chief Marketing Officer for Uncle Ben's, an African American man, agreed.

100 scripts and 6 months worth of casting later, we found ourselves shooting a dozen commercials on a sound stage in Culver City. These were not expensive commercials. But they weren't inexpensive either. Sadly, no one will ever see them. Because a week before they were due to air, the client shelved the whole project.

Despite testing extremely well in focus groups, the client caved in to pressure from special interest groups. Even though we were trying to right a wrong, these groups claimed the CEO character was offensive. They said we should have given Ben a last name. And that we should have put him in a better suit, without the bow tie.

Really? A last name and a sport coat would have fixed everything?

At one point we had discussed an Armani suit, but the client thought we would have to change all the packaging. And that could get quite costly. We even suggested dropping Uncle from the name. Or changing Uncle Ben from an African American man to a caucasian man, thus eliminating any controversy whatsoever.

But in the mixed up world of racial arithmetic, those ideas were met by objections as well.

And so what was offensive before, was never corrected. Or even addressed. And to this day it remains patently offensive. But apparently it's less offensive than it would have been had we made Ben a Chief Executive Officer.

It appears we don't live in a post-racial world.

Perhaps we never will.

Pass the potatoes.

Hello Advertising

This story is going to sound very familiar to you.

It wasn't inspired by any specific set of circumstances that happened to a colleague within the last month. Six months. Or even a year. Because the truth is, it has happened to me. And it has happened to you. And if it hasn't happened to you, trust me it will.

You take on a new job.

You're excited.

And you've got a hard-on for the business.

Doesn't have to be advertising, but for the sake of this piece let's say it is.

You dig in, drink the Kool Aid and devote yourself to the craft. That means taking on a leadership role. Not only voicing a strong opinion but doing the homework and the legwork to back it up. It can be a grind. You eat a tiny bowl of shit once in a while. And you bite your tongue when you have to.

But it's all for the good of the team. And the agency.

A year or two later, you start to see the fruits of your labor. Business picks up. You notch a few pitch victories. And get some decent TV spots out the door....oh, I'm sorry, Integrated Branded Content Units.

All the hard work has paid off. Or at least, in theory, it should.

Because the closed-door, throbbing-vein meeting with the agency CEO did not go as well as you had hoped.

"We'd like to give you a promotion, we really would. And we'd like to give you a bump in salary, but we really can't. I know we had discussed the idea of incentives and bonuses when we first hired you, but as you know, we've all had to tighten our belts."

Really? We've all had to tighten our belts? Then why am I picking up the Wall St. Journal and reading about a 43% pay hike for the holding company officers?

Why is Business Insider doing a photo shoot of the coolest vacation homes belonging to the 37 Wealthiest Ad Pros? 23 of whom work for this organization?

And how does the agency afford your three times a week in-office Bikram Yoga Sessions?

"Company policy says you're not supposed to be reading the Wall St. Journal, Business Insider, Adweek, Adage, or Mediabistro. Agency employees are also requested not to look at any SEC filings or publicly disclosed financial documents. And under no circumstances are agency staff permitted to read the heretical writings at RoundSeventeen."

And so you do what any disgruntled employee would do.

But you never get out of the car at the gun store parking lot. And instead start interviewing with another agency. They are impressed with your achievements and make you an offer you can't refuse.

Not without some delicious feeling of delight, you give your two week notice.

And suddenly, the belt that was supposed to be tightened, miraculously becomes loose. Especially after the agency does the calculations and decides it would cost more to replace you than to properly butter your bread as they originally promised.

Too late, you tell them.
And rightfully so.

If this has happened once, it's happened a million times. It's happening right now.

Some mid-level creative has sweated all weekend long to build up the courage and request a chat with the CCO or CEO. And even as you are reading this, some muckutty-muck is hemming and hawing his or her way through a convoluted monetary discussion that boils down to:

"There's plenty for us, there's none for you."

When I am asked to give advice to younger people, you

know younger than 44, I always tell them to strike while the metal is hot.

If you are lucky enough to hit a home run in this business or even knock out a few triples with players in scoring position, you must immediately translate that into some form of compensation.

Now. Do not take "no" for answer.

Because the people you are working for, the ones telling you there is no money, these are the same people who are capitalizing on your success. They're slapping their names on the credit list. They're sitting on panels, bloviating about their imaginary contribution to the idea. They're having private conversations with their bosses. They're asking for more money.

And guess what, they're getting it.

"Siegel, you've got to go home."

"We're ordering food, do you want some?"

I do want food.

But I don't want to eat it here with you slobs. I don't want to watch you assemble a 259 page deck. And I definitely don't want to be here when the big cheese gets the PDF at home and starts barking changes just as Jimmy Fallon signs off the air later tonight.

I want to go home. I want to change out of these "business" clothes, lift some weights, jump on the elliptical I have in my garage, and then set my fat ass in front of the TV where I can slaughter the contestants at Jeopardy, drink beer and pretend to listen to my wife.

That's what I want.

And if you, Mr. or Mrs. Agency Big Wig had any inkling about creative management or even took Psych 101 in college, you'd insist I unplug my laptop and head for the door.

Years ago, I heard an anecdote about a legendary freelance writer whose name I will not mention because it's a little embarrassing to place the word legendary next to the word copywriter.

Louis Zamperini was a legend. Some schmuck who writes

an Oreo tweet during a Super Bowl is not a legend.

Anyway, this anonymous writer famously told a hardballing recruiter, "If you can't afford my day rate, you can't afford me." I love that. He also said, "Don't expect any new ideas after 4 PM."

He wasn't being rude.
Or short.
He was being honest.

Maybe it's a writer thing, but we are at our best in the morning. If I'm brain deep in a challenge I will often wake up with half-formed ideas already in my head. If it's a manifesto type thing, or long copy or even headlines, I've got 500 or so words strung out in my cerebellum before I've stepped out of the shower.

By the time the hipsters in their skinny jeans and Pharrell hats come strolling in, I'm already mapping out a second campaign.

I'm not being immodest, but I'm 44 now and I know what works best for me.

And I know what works best for you, Mr. or Mrs. Potential Employer.

You're paying me a handsome day rate.
To write.

You're not paying me to manage. Or sit through meetings. Or navigate office politics. You're paying me to come up with ideas and write. Extending my normal day into a torturous night of flip flopping, strategic changes, and deck assembling is robbing me of my routine. A routine that allows me to unwind, recharge and refresh.

In other words you can squeeze me for all I'm worth today, but tomorrow I'll be as worthless as a Zune.

It's all about efficiency and cost-to-work ratios.

The smart employer will come looking for me at 5:30 PM and tell me to hit the high road.

The really smart employer will already be in my face at 3:59 PM.

Funny is No Longer Money

Last week I was paid one of the highest, though useless, compliments I've ever heard.

A friend and competitive copywriting colleague, stated in his review of my last book, *Round Seventeen &1/2, The Names Have Been Changed to Protect the Inefficient:...*

"Rich is the first freelance copywriter I would hire if I needed to write something funny."

High praise, right?

The problem is, nobody seems to need something funny.

When was the last time you saw something truly funny on TV? Or heard something funny on the radio? Or read something funny in a magazine (dinosaur alert)? OK, came across something funny on the interwebs?

I'll wait.

You see, with the exception of Wieden & Kennedy, the absurdist fare from Gerry Graf and the unbeatable deadpan delivery by Blake Griffin in those Kia spots, it seems laughter is no longer in vogue.

Today brands are all about attaching themselves to causes.

As if corporate altruism were some magic panacea.

"When you buy a Carrier Central Air Conditioning unit, we'll donate a nickel to the Feed the Children Foundation. So now you can feel good about feeling good."

There's also a lot of tear-jerking going around.

"Your assignment today is to craft a 2 minute short viral film that will tug at our target audience's heartstrings and make them feel different about our Monroe Shock Absorbers."

And finally, there's this unfounded belief that brands can be built online, for no money, by offering consumers a warehouse-sized toy store of Frivolous, Fuckwadian Digital Knick Knacks™.

"Upload your headshot and Kelloggs will turn you into a Lucky Charm."

As recently as last year, I was brought in to an agency to come up with a sharp, observational humor campaign for a huge beer account. Work that had the same vibe as our earlier ABC campaign. So that's what I gave them.

I wasn't around for the presentation but I'm told the client thought the work was, "too smart."

I've seen what they put on the air. And I'm proud to say that client was 100% right.

If funny ever comes back, you know where to reach me.
I'll be at my keyboard whoring this book.

Or my last one.

It's Just Business

I'm not a trucker hat kind of guy.

I'll wear a baseball cap on occasion, mostly to shield my bald head from the sun, but you'll never see me sporting one of those branded, douchy, flat-brimmed Ashton Kutsher caps.

I know this borders on heresy, particularly since the marketing of brands has put a roof over my head, clothes on my children's back, food on the dinner table and has even given me the opportunity to fly 4,000 miles where I could sit on a Tulum beach and stare at reddish-brown seaweed.

But I don't love brands.

And chunks of past-eaten burritos always come bubbling up when I hear fellow colleagues blather on about how they do.

I wonder if these same brandaphiles also agree with the Supreme Court that corporations are people too.

Maybe it's because I never dreamed of a career in advertising.

I sort of fell into it. And discovered it was a great way to make a living while exercising my desire to write. A great lucrative way, that has sustained me well into my mid 40's.

Granted, there are brands that I have liked considerably more than others. Mostly because they were willing to go out on a limb with me and my partners and let us swing for the fences. Those include ABC, Castlemaine XXXX, Bizrate, homestore, Earthlink, Acura, and Baikalskaya Vodka.

But as Sal Tessio tells Michael Corleone before he is taken away to be shot for his betrayal...

"Tell Mikey, I always liked him. It was always just business, nothing personal."

Thankfully, I am not, and never was, one of those creative directors sought out by the press for interviews. So I never had to drop to my knees and flap my lips about loving a brand, or their DNA, or their undeniable authenticity, or their invaluable contribution to mankind.

If on the other hand, some probing reporter were to ask me if there were any brands I hate, I'd be more than willing to oblige, starting with:

Time Warner Cable

Comcast

American Airlines (or any other airline)

Dell Computers

Pabst Blue Ribbon Beer

Sit N' Sleep

IKEA

Random House Publishing

Outback Steakhouse

Chevy's Mexican Restaurants

I better stop there, before I step on any toes.

That's Dead

I am now sliding into my third voluntary week away from
work. I am afforded this because this past year has been
unusually busy. Perhaps the busiest in my dozen years as a
freelancing mercenary.

I'm seeing a lot of articles lately about ageism. Maybe
people don't know I'm an over-ripe 44 years of age.

In any case, I'm not complaining.
Ok, I am complaining.

You see over the course of the last 12 months I've written
hundreds of scripts, penned another 50 concepts for digital,
laid down a bunch of manifestos and even cranked out a
few banner ads. That is, I've come up with ideas for all of the
above.

None of it got produced.

Not a single one.

This all became painfully apparent when, the other night
at an Angels baseball game, my nephew asked me what
television commercials I had on the air right now. I
stammered, took a sip of my $13 Coors Light and quickly
changed the subject.

"You want another ice cream popsicle?"

I don't have anything on the air. And haven't for a while. The last time I produced anything President Bush was standing on an aircraft carrier and my shares of MCI Worldcom had suddenly become toilet paper.

Look, when it comes to ideas, I shit the bed as much as the next guy. Mine are just a little more expensive. Similarly, and not to sound immodest, once in every 50 at bats or so, I can hit one out of the park. In fact, on one recent assignment I'm sure my partner and I had done just that.

The specifics are unimportant. The agency, the client, the creative directors can all rest assured I'm not going to divulge any details.

But I've been around the block. A few times. I've judged shows. Picked up a few awards here and there. I've pitched and won new business. And had the great fortune to work side by side with legends in the business.

I know a good ad when I see one. Or written one.

This one was good. And could've been great. Not because it was mine, it wasn't. It was a true collaboration where my partner said one thing, I said another, he said something else. I ignored that. Then tweaked the 30th thing he said. And voilà, the spot was born.

It was pure.
It was simple.
It was funny.

And it was based on a human truth that everyone will recognize. Or would have.

But now it's dead.

Why? Because in the assemblage of a 279-page deck, it somehow got lost in the shuffle. Passed over for some nonsense with a cool hippety-hoppity soundtrack or a buzz worthy brand engagement unit that was not buzz worthy in the least.

I don't think a client ever saw it. I don't think the lead creative director ever saw it. In its final indignity, the paper the idea was printed on never even made it to the recycle bin. It got tossed in with the trash and quickly smothered with last night's cold Pad Thai Noodle.

Want to know why 99% of the advertising on TV sucks?

It's because 99% of the great ideas never make it out the door.

We Gotta Have a Movement.

There was a time in advertising –uh-oh, old man on warpath again – when the goal was to move the merchandise. If we could help the client raise sales figures 3.6 %, 7.1% or 9.4%, we were doing our job.

And doing it well.

And barring the hiring of a new Chief Marketing Officer, we could expect to be retained for another torturous year.

Then, someone got it in their head that we needed to "engage" the consumer.

Through the magic of social media we could have ongoing "dialog" with the people buying our enamel-strengthening toothpaste or twice-baked wheat crackers.

If we reached them with enough touchpoints, the thinking goes, we could actually have a long-lasting, meaningful "conversation" with the folks who wipe their asses with our 4-ply quilted toilet paper.

But that was not sufficient.
Soon, we were asked to go "viral."

Write, craft, design and cobble together a long form video – with $80,000 – that once uploaded onto a free YouTube channel, will spread like wildfire and threaten to dethrone Justin Bieber or that cello-playing cat.

A tall order.
But not the tallest.

Because now there is rarely a brief that crosses my desk, and
when I say desk I mean picnic table set up for the freelancers,
or pops up in a PDF via email, when I'm lucky enough to
work at home, that does not include the delusional
instructive to "create a worldwide movement."

A Movement!

You see it's not enough that we sell more Craftsmen Staple
Guns or Toyota Scions or Arby's French Dip Manwiches,
now it's our responsibility to turn those converted sales into
brand evangelists.

To get them off their duffs and into the streets. Marching
with uncontainable enthusiasm and nothing more important
to do with their time than to get others onboard and spread
the love of their new Hefty Stretchable Trash Bags.

It simply defies all manner of logic and common sense.

It has taken me 20 years and I still can't convince my
daughters to make their beds or put the dishes in the
dishwasher. But now, and for no apparent reason, you want
me to persuade people that your new Parkay Butter is so
good and clings to bread so well, they should eat their toast
upside down?

And you want me to do it with a 76 X 128 banner ad?

Got it.

I'll show you where I'm at in 6 hours.

Oh, silly me, 3 hours.

A Monkey Can Do It.

Unlike some of my more demure colleagues, I have no problem questioning the wisdom of a strategic brief, or its author, the planner. And why should I? After all, they question the validity of our work on a weekly basis.

Did I say weekly? I meant daily.

Because God knows creatives, even seasoned veterans like myself, don't have the wherewithal to move forward and develop an advertising campaign without the daily watchful guidance and skilled expertise of a professional planner with degrees in...what is it they have degrees in?

Point being, I've heard some awful stupid stuff from the planning department.

Years ago, we were pitching Sparklett's Water and to the credit of the crack research team and the careful analysis of all the big data, the planner had successfully reduced the strategy down to its barest minimum. Not one page mind you, one word.

BLUE.

That's right, we, the cynics and jaded artisans in the creative department, were told to vigorously pursue and make hay out of the word BLUE.

Years later, I was working at a different agency, and I use the word different hesitantly because they're different in name only, and I balked at a different brief. I don't even remember what it was for, nor is it important. The sheer fact that I dared to question the logic of the brief brought about a completely unexpected response...

"Rich, I'll grant you that it's not the most insightful brief in the world, but they all can't be as brilliant as Got Milk? It just doesn't work that way."

Well, there's a new benchmark for underachievement. They all can't be Apple's *1984* or VW's *Darth Vader*, I thought, but that doesn't mean we don't try.

Recently I sat in on a meeting and heard the latest nugget for my collection. And this is one my fellow copywriters can savor for years. A planner was heard to say...

"If we get the brief right, the spots will literally write themselves."

Good thing this happened early in the morning and I was on an empty stomach, because had it transpired a few hours later in the day, I would have seen my lunch for the second time.

Spots do not write themselves.
Nor do they rewrite themselves after the brief has changed.

Nor do they rewrite the rewrites because someone in upper management doesn't like dogs. Or umbrellas. Or ketchup.

Or seven. Or tweed. Or convertibles. Or love seats. Or oranges.

If it ever gets to a point where spots do write themselves, I'll be out of a job.

Of course, I could go into planning, how hard can that be?

Selling by Unselling.

It isn't often that I get to blather on about advertising genius; lately those two words have become an oxymoron.

More surprisingly, I, nor any of my immediate colleagues, had anything to do with the brilliance of which I am about to speak.

Last week, REI announced they would not be opening their doors for Black Friday, the consummate day of shopping after Thanksgiving that often involves random bloody violence, gluttonous consumerism, and long lines of eager buyers camped out in a parking lot with the hope of scoring a 40% discount on a cheap Chinese-made toaster oven.

In other words, the trifecta of modern American culture.

But REI – the leading purveyor of outdoor activity equipment – will have none of that.

While others are zigging, they are zagging. Or in the parlance of mountaineers, they are *abseiling* while others are *jumaring*.

Some retailers are following suit and shuttering their doors, but REI, more likely someone at REI's advertising/PR agency told them to make a big stink out of the deal. Because – and this is the genius part – it played right into the brand's creedo to get people outside more often.

By forfeiting whatever revenue would normally come in on that day, they would more than make up for it in the 364 other days of the year when their name had been firmly cemented as the go-to place for legitimate sporting equipment.

Not to mention all the free publicity the story generated.

Full disclosure: I am an REI Club Member and pre-disposed to like this brand. Before my yearly camping trips, my wife and I can be found scouring the aisles of the local outlet. She, for new camping outfits. Me, for some clever new device that will eliminate the need to get out of the tent when nature and my overactive bladder calls.

Let me digress with a slightly similar tale.

Years ago, my partner and I were asked to lead the pitch for Hardee's, or as we referred to them, the shoe-less, biscuit-baking Appalachian cousin to Carl's Jr.

For research purposes, we flew to Alabama or Mississippi or one of the Jew-hating states to sample the goods. It wasn't good.

The food sucked.
But the place where the food was sold, sucked even more.
I've been in more attractive service station restrooms.

We had this crazy idea: we would walk into the pitch for the $40 million account and tell Hardee's to cut their advertising budget in half. Then, as responsible brand stewards, we would suggest they funnel that $20 million into operations: cleaning up the stores, fixing the broken equipment, and firing the employees who had all the enthusiasm of a three-toed sloth.

How refreshing it would be for a client to hear an ad agency forego half the billings for the better long term interests of the company?

Maybe it was because negotiations were still under way with the holding company or maybe it was because it was 4 PM on a kegger Friday afternoon when we brought the idea up with our agency "management" but that idea went nowhere fast.

"Are you kidding? That's about 2 million in revenue. I spent that much money on rosé wine at Cannes last year. Why don't you try to do something funny with their star?"

We didn't win the business. And for bringing up similar boat-rocking ideas and for being contrarian in general, my partner and I were shown the door.

None of which helped the Hardee's brand.

But in retrospect, 'getting quit' and no longer having to work for Captain Hazelwood, was the best thing that ever happened to me.

Read This. Now. Damnit.

Nuance and client feedback appear to be mutually exclusive these days.

When I do hear from clients it's rarely:

"Could the joke be a little more pointed?"

Or

"It's feels flat, could we give it another twist?

Or

"The strategy called for something innovative and different, could this be different in a groundbreaking sort of way?"

It's never like that.

If there is any feedback, and many times there isn't, there's simply the ripping up of one brief in exchange for a hastily-composed other brief, or it goes along the lines of:

"It has to be more urgent. URGENT!!!!!!"

That's advertising today. Tear jerking spots and digital toys that sell nothing. Or hard-hitting, retail, Tier Five ads that have to sell everything.

EVERYTHING!!!

It doesn't matter if it's for cars, pizza, beer, or a phone company, the tail that wags the dog is the CTA.

The Call To Action.

Clients want it louder. They want it stronger. They want the call to action at the beginning of a spot, in the middle of a spot and at the end of the spot. If it weren't for the pesky product or service, they'd have the call to action *be* the spot.

They must know something I don't.

Because in all my dealings with a salesperson, I've never found myself convinced by someone yelling at me. Or annoying me. Or getting up in my face, so close that I can tell what they had for breakfast. Last week.

It's as if today's advertisers believe they can bully consumers into buying their crap.

And of course no one on the agency side wants to tell them otherwise because frankly, "if your agency won't get on the bullhorn and corral the sheeple into our abattoir, we'll find one, with a lower retainer fee, that will."

I miss the days when advertising was about the art of persuasion. Of pinpointing a unique position in the marketplace. And finding smart, subtle ways to convince consumers that no other brand was worthy of their attention.

We used long copy to cajole people, to inform them, and

bring them around to a brand's point of view.

We used TV and radio – remember radio – to charm folks. Monday mornings at the office used to include water cooler chat about some funny spot someone had seen over the weekend. When was the last time you heard someone say,

"Hey did you see that new Tostitos commercial?"

We used creativity as a tool. And the agencies that had the better toolboxes were easily distinguishable from the ones that didn't.

That pecking order has all but disappeared. It's not unusual to see Droga 5 pitching the same piece of business as the Zimmerman Agency.

In fact, in the year 2016, I'd give the edge to the latter, because no one does a CTA better than they do. When the FTC relaxes language restrictions on advertising, and I'm convinced they will, the folks in Florida will be the first to drop the F-bomb in an ad.

"Get your fuckin' asses down here, before I come to your fuckin' house and punch your fuckin' lights out."

Client: That's good. Can you add 'today' or 'now' to the copy? You know, so it feels more urgent.

I'm Outtahere.

There was a great piece that was widely published recently. It's written by an art director, usually not a good sign, but in this case it's the exception.

The author offers his unique perspective on life in advertising and the unusual demands it made on his cancer-shortened life.

Thankfully, I'm in excellent health and therefore cannot muster that type of depth and insight. However I did spend many of my years working at Chiat/Day when it earned its moniker Chiat/Day & Night and have my own opinions on the matter of burning the midnight oil.

I simply didn't do it.

I worked late on occasion, sometimes until 7 or 7:30. And I came in on the weekends for new business pitches, particularly when Lee Clow and Bob Kuperman were there.

But by and large I went home at a decent hour and spent time with my family – though I'm sure there were times my wife and my daughters wished I had stayed the office.

Did this impede my career progress?

Probably.

But truth be told I had no interest in palling around with

upper management at 10 PM just for the sake of appearing like a good company man. And to be completely honest, I never developed the acquired taste for Kool Aid.

I prefer to think that my slow advancement was due more to my opinionated opinions and the unfiltered expression of those opinions. In fact, I'm sure there were times many of my colleagues wished I had gone home earlier.

But wait, there's more. You see, I also happen to be a big believer in The Law of Diminishing Returns.

Working late never increased the probability of coming up with the big idea. It reduced it.

Besides, unlike other creatives, I don't mosey in to work at 11 o'clock in the morning. I get in at a decent hour and I make with the funny right away.

I don't spend a lot of time cavorting or chatting up it with other employees like it's high school. I put my considerable nose to the grindstone and keep it there until 5.

Or 5:30, depending on my caffeine intake.

In the end, as the now-deceased author says, it's all just advertising.

TV commercials, print ads, websites, and mobile apps, that are utterly disposable. I've never conflated advertising to be anything more than that. It's simply a way to put food on my family's table. Never to be confused with anything lasting or meaningful.

That, I'll save for my novel.

Shaking in the Bush, Boss.

It might happen today.

It might happen tomorrow.

But there can be no doubt, it will happen soon.

A Fortune 500 company will put out a press release announcing an advertising agency review.

"We have been extremely satisfied with _____, _____ & _____. Their creative execution and strategic insight have been impeccable and have served us well for more than 32 years. However, with the changing social media landscape and the emergence of new global markets we feel compelled to trash this relationship, ignore the loyalty and explore all options. We look forward to being wined, dined and in some cases, provided with mounds of cocaine and expensive escorts."

This will set off an all-too-familiar chain of events.

There will be blood in the water.

The holding company warlords will move their pieces around, figuring out the best point of attack.

Motivational staff memos will be written. With empty promises of fame, glory and wealth. Because let's remember, no one gets bonuses or raises until the bosses get paid.

And finally, vacations, those much-needed breaks from the demoralizing grind that is advertising today, will be canceled.

Thanksgiving won't be spent sitting around the fireplace, watching the Detroit Lions lose and eating turkey, cranberry sauce and pumpkin pie.

Thanksgiving will be spent at the cubicle farm. With cold coffee and muttering co-workers. Although some overly-perky assistant, who mistakenly believes she can turn those frowns upside down, will bring in special Thanksgiving pizza, topped with turkey, and other unfit-for-pizza toppings.

And Christmas?

Well, that's sacred. So agency bosses will insist everybody leave the office by 9 PM on Christmas Eve. And not come in until noon on Christmas Day.

You know, just like last year.

New Year's Day is when millions of Americans make their resolutions and vow to change the habits that have blackened their lungs, rotted their livers or chewed through their nasal membranes.

In that spirit of change, the all-knowing powers that be in the agency world will ditch the brief everyone has been working against for the last two months and proclaim, with no hint of irony, "we have a new strategic direction."

If you sense I'm grumbling, you're not reading this correctly.

As a staff guy, this annual ritual would make my blood boil.

But as an atheist freelancer with no regard for the holidays and an insatiable desire to work, this kind of nonsense only makes my Stay-Out-Of-A-Dirty-Nursing-Home-Retirement account swell.

For me, this really is The Most Wonderful Time of the Year.

Pass the Mushu Pork, Please

If I were to ever own my own ad agency, and I've threatened such a scenario for years, the scope of services would be very limited.

1. We would make the ads.
2. We would manage the creation, production and distribution of the ads.
3. And then we would bill the client.

We would operate this way, not because those are the only areas where I have some expertise, but because anything else is superfluous.

Of course, that is NOT the general direction in which most agencies are going. And I should know, I have worked in all of them.

These days the scope of services goes way beyond the making of ads. Agencies today are more than willing to tell clients, and sell clients, profound insights as to what goes into making a culture.

A few weeks ago, I was working out of the cafeteria of a company that shall remain anonymous – "The names have been changed to protect the inefficient."

There, I had the distinct pleasure of eavesdropping in on a "business" conversation by the planners. I believe they are now called Cultural Experiential Anthropologists.

It was all so enlightening. Had you squinted your eyes and employed a little cognitive dissonance you would have sworn you were in the living room of the local Tri-Delt House.

"So, let's talk about emoticons."
"OMG, I hate emoticons."
"Hello, 2007 called and it wants its winky face back."
"Know what's worse than emoticons? Acroynms."
"Yeah. I can't stand acronyms."
"OMG, me too!" (from one assistant who was impossibly more clueless than the others)
"How many of you have ever Instagrammed a meal before?"
"Speaking of meals, look somebody just put leftover birthday cake on the counter."

By the way, I may be a hardcore atheist but I would put my hand on a Bible/Torah/Quran, or even Darwin's *The Origin of a Species*, and swear the dialogue quoted above is a true word-for-word accounting.

At the conclusion of this Insight Farming Session (OK, that I made up, but I'm sure they had some jargon-y term for what had just transpired) somebody volunteered to compile all the "findings."

I'm sure a deck was made.
An invoice was generated.

And a check was blindly written by the client to pay for this groundbreaking research.

I can't help wondering how many doohickees/whatchama-callits/thiggamajigs the client has to sell just to cover this cost of this horse hockey.

I may not possess an MBA. Or a sophisticated knowledge of human behavior and the changing dynamics of a fractured media landscape. And I lack the ability to discern the intricate differences between a 'Pragmatic Charismatic' and a 'Practical Self-Actualizer.'

But this, the above tale, is what passes for marketing and business acumen in the halls of corporate America in the year 2016.

And it explains why in 50 years we're all going to be speaking Mandarin.

The Freelancer's Owner Manual

Today I'm talking to my people.

No, not grumpy old Jews with an unlimited supply of righteous indignation and a garage full of soapboxes.

I'm talking about art directors and copywriters, of the freelance variety.

Right now, there are more advertising freelancers than I have ever seen in my entire career. There isn't a day that goes by that I don't receive a phone call, a text or an email to the effect of,

"Hey, Rich if you know of any gigs out there send me your overflow."

Ok, that's not entirely true – those requests never come via a phone call.

The point is, there are a lot of us creative mercenaries. And I don't think that's bad for ad agencies. In fact, as I have pointed out many times before, I believe it can be good. Very, very good.

As a public service to ad agencies all across this great land as well as those on the other side of the Greenwich Line (because I occasionally go international), I'd like to offer up some helpful hints in what I'm calling:

The Care and Feeding of Your Freelancer

1. **Be Prepared** – Years ago, I was hired for a long term project at a rather obscene day rate. I won't say the name of the company but it rhymes with Zapple. I arrived on a Monday morning, ready to dazzle the Zapple people with my creative wares. But the brief was not ready until Thursday. That's three full wasted day rates. Look, I'm happy to take your money, cruise internet memes and pore through photos of Kim Jung Un all day long, but after a while Jewish guilt sets in. We freelancers want to work. Just tell us what the ideas are supposed to be about.

2. **Give Us Time** – Over the last dozen years, I've been brought in countless times to reposition a brand. This is a monumental task. And it doesn't happen in the span of one rotation of the earth. *"Here's the brief, let's see where you're at tomorrow morning."* Look, I wasn't in the room at Chiat/Day when they came up with Think Different and Here's to the Crazy Ones, and by the way it's shameful how many people are claiming credit for that work, but I was down the hall when it came into being. And I can tell you it didn't happen overnight. Or overweek. Or even overmonth.

3. **Fewer Meetings, More Work** – It goes without saying that if you've hired a freelancer you're paying a premium for what you hope to receive are solid solutions. What you don't want to be doing is paying top dollar to a bunch of fidgety creatives who are inordinately averse to PowerPoint decks, marketing-speak, and incomprehensible intersecting rhomboids and trapezoids. Wink, wink, we hate trapezoids.

4. **Lay off the Layers** – If there's one thing we've learned

from Washington DC and our inept members of Congress, it's that bureaucracy and politics produce more bureaucracy and more politics. Nothing good ever came out of GroupThink, with the possible exception of Windows 95™. Freelancers want nothing more than to do the work. We have no hidden agendas. No ambition. And no desire to move up the company org chart. Hell, we don't even want to look at a company org chart. It's why we became freelancers in the first place.

5. **The Long Leash** – My dog is 13 years old, pushing 14. When I take her out for a walk I put her on the leash. The truth is, I don't have to. She doesn't pull ahead, as she did when she was a pup. She doesn't bolt across the street to chase squirrels. She simply walks by my side and obeys all my commands. It's the benefit of experience. Similarly, most freelancers tend to be on the older side. Not 44 like me, but they've been around the block. You can depend on them. They're going to get the work done. Whether it's offsite or onsite. Or a flexible combination of both. Of course, if you want them onsite, it's always a good idea to have free food around. We are by nature, cheap dates.

6. **1099 Us** – I'm no accountant, though I come from a long line of CPA's, but I can't tell you the exuberant joy that courses through my body when, prior to booking a gig, an HR person will ask, "Is it OK if we 1099 you?" OK? I'll slash my day rate to get a full 1099 paycheck. I'll gladly let my crafty accountant sort through the tax code and get me deductions for everything from my oven roasted turkey sandwiches (eaten while working) to my new Shimano FSX

Mountain Bike (ridden while ideating.) Note: we also hate the word *ideating.*

With the possible exception of the last tip, all these tips are guaranteed to increase the bottom line of ad agencies hiring freelancers.

And really, isn't that what it's all about? Making more money for the holding companies.

I'm going to stop here at 6 points. I know that's an odd number and doesn't fit into the common listicle format of 5 or even 10. But that's exactly the kind of reckless and irresponsible freedom that makes life worth living as an advertising freelancer.

Pinch Me.

Last week I had one of those mystical media moments.

You know the ones. You read a headline on an article. You're sucked in by its intriguing content. You comb through the entire piece, thinking "this is too good to be true." So you check the identity of the publisher. See that it's a satirical site. Slam your fist on the desk and realize, "yes, I've been fooled again, a victim of my own gullibility and the internet's surprising ability to make even the most amateurish journalism appear legit."

That almost happened to me.
But then, it didn't.

Wieden & Kennedy in London shocked the agency world when they announced their efforts to give their employees a better work/life balance. This of course is a misnomer because if you work a staff job in advertising, the balance is more accurately described by work/self-loathing.

Nevertheless, they revealed their plan to ban meetings before 10 AM as well as after 4 PM. They've also instructed workers to stop reading emails past 7 PM.

As you know, I'm a card-carrying member of the United Jeopardy Watchers, Local #537. And have long advocated the reinstatement of normal business hours.

I'm a firm believer that you will not get any good ideas out of me past 5 PM. And keeping me late tonight only reduces my alleged 'productivity' for tomorrow.

In fact, I believe I've broached this topic many times in the past. The narcissist in me wants to believe that yes. Finally. People are listening to this old goat.

I've stood on this homemade soapbox and railed against the abuses dished out daily by a merciless world and now my whiny, grumpy voice is being heard. If all goes according to plan, it won't be long before we see the end of the Open Office. Or the endless battalions of planners, planners, and more planners.

As Jimmy McGill of *Better Call Saul* would say, "The headline here is: 44-Year Old Curmudgeon Sparks the Return of Common Sense."

The realist in me must always smack the narcissist upside the head, reminding him that if anyone were actually listening, the RoundSeventeen blog might actually turn a dime and earn enough money for at least a scone and latte at a local Starbucks. But it hasn't.

What's happening, and I like to believe this is widespread, is that ad agencies have unexpectedly unearthed the Law of Diminishing Returns.

Here are a few axioms of the LDR:

The more overtime your employees put in,
the less the quality of their output.

The more people involved in a decision,
the less the likelihood of making a good one.

The more weekends you steal from your people,
the less the probability you have of seeing those same people at
the year end Christmas Party.

I hope the pendulum is swinging the other way. In the
direction of agencies treating their employees more humanely.
By being more efficient. By learning to say "No" to abusive
clients. And by respecting the boundaries between work
and life.

Particularly since, despite my best attempts to dissuade her,
my daughter has recently expressed an interest in entering the
agency world.

It's not enough that advertising has permanently scarred my
wife and I, now it's going after my children.

Steam 'em and Gleam 'em.

I've often said, "it's harder to do bad advertising than it is to do good." And I don't know if you've noticed lately, but there is a lot of bad advertising out there. I've been watching the NCAA basketball tournament, so I know.

There's the couple who are so averse to talking about their retirement plans they go to extreme lengths *not* to talk about it. The wife purposely messes up the windows. The man busts the gutter and throws his car keys over the fence. Oh the hilarity.

There's another cloying version of the McPick Two jingle.

And there's car porn. Lots of car porn. On beautiful, dimly lit urban streets. On windy mountain roads. And streaking across desert flats. All accompanied with the worst voiceover copy that seems to have been written by a brain dead committee of twelve.

I don't have anything on the air, but I'm just as guilty for polluting corporate boardrooms as anyone else. It's how I put food on my family's dinner table.

If I had an agency I'd call it: **Decks and Checks**™.

What makes bad advertising so difficult is that it starts out bad – mostly because the client has asked for something bad – trying to cram 10 lbs. of horse shit into a bag clearly designed for only 5 lbs. of horse shit.

And then it only gets worse. There are meetings. Revisions. More meetings. More horse shit.

And then, when the turd has been finely polished, it is offered up before the Media Department, the new overlords of the advertising kingdom.

"These are great, but we only bought 15 second spots. Can you make these work in 15 seconds?"

Of course we can. Because we are professionals. We see problems as opportunities. And we relish a good challenge.

I'd like a different kind of challenge.

For once I'd like a Creative Director to look over the work, turn to me and say, "Can you push it even further? Can you give it more edge? Can you increase the tension and make this thing – could be a spot, a print piece, or even a digital idea – more impactful? Can you do that Mr. Creative Guy?"

But, as a fellow trench-dweller, you know that's not what happens. The changes we're asked to make are of a more mundane nature.

"The client doesn't like the word, tangy. Or, plus. Or, affordable."

"We don't have the budget for an elephant, can it be a very large dog?"

"Can you say the name of the product in the first 6 seconds?"

When I started writing this blog, I jokingly named it RoundSeventeen as a hat tip to the ridiculous number of changes we need to make in order to get a Skip Ad on the air. Or on a YouTube pre-roll.

Seventeen seemed excessive. And properly connoted the dysfunctional nature of the creative process.

That was way back in 2009.

Today, a piece of work can go through 17 rounds of revisions before I take my noontime swim.

A Plethora of Recruiters

Today's topic: Recruiters.

Why the hell are there so many recruiters?

Have you been on linkedin.com lately?

Sandwiched between newsfeed items asking me to name a city without the letter A – how about Asshattery, Arkansas?

Or to solve some inane mathematical equation – again I'm going with Asshattery, Arkansas, there's a new announcement from someone entering the new lucrative field of recruiting.

I'm not here to disparage recruiters.

I've been known to bite the hand that feeds me but I'm not into full blown self-destruction mode (yet) and I still get the occasional employment booking through friends who are recruiters – you long-timers in Los Angeles know who you are.

And that I love you dearly.

I'm simply questioning the sudden explosion. It's like the 17 year cycle of the cicada. Only now the woodworks are clogged up with recruiters. It seems like everyone and their pilates instructor is in the recruiting game.

Moment of serendipity, and this is the absolute truth, as I am

writing this and mapping the next paragraph in my head, I
received an email informing me of my newest linkedin
connection – a recruiter.

All of which begs the question.

Why are organizations having such a difficult time getting
people to come through the front door? I'm just winging it
here, but it may have a little to do with the sweatshop
reputation many agencies wear so proudly on their $200
flannel sleeves.

Or the fact that the pay scale sucks, with holding company
CEO's often "earning" 800 times what the lowest employee
on ad agency ladder makes. By the way, that lowest rung
occupier usually goes by the title of Associate Creative Director.

Or, that the quality of work coming out of ad agencies simply
does not merit the time nor the reward nor the free Chicken
Tikka Masala brought in every night to feed the masses.

More importantly, what specific jobs are these communication
pros recruiting for? Is there a boom coming to the marketing
world that will propel the industry forward and bring about
a new golden age of advertising?

Oh... silly me, I just answered my question.

Planners.

An agency can never have enough planners.

Cutting All the Wrong Corners

Years ago, I did a TV shoot in Coral Cables, Florida. My
art director partner wanted a pinkish dusk sky with big
bulbous booming clouds in the background. This was
before Photoshop, InDesign or CGI rendering, and so the
only buttons we could push were the ones on the telephone.

To call the travel agent.

We were in Florida for a week. At one of Miami's swankiest
hotels. We ate at Joe's Stone Crab. And after a hectic morning
of tech scouting, we lazed around on a yacht that sailed us
by Key Largo. The chef onboard made us sandwiches, fruit
cocktails and little fancy appetizers one normally sees at a
Bar Mitzvah or a wedding.

Those lavish days are long gone.

Now every production (at every ad agency) comes under the
scrutiny of hard-nosed cost control consultants who nickel
and dime every line item until they've separated the boon
from the doogle.

*"Oh you want two 10K lighting packages? I think you can do
it with one"*

*"That A-list director would be nice, but this fellow is cheaper.
Did you see the campaign he did for Sizzler?"*

"We can't afford the Sheraton, unless the agency creatives share rooms. There's a Red Roof Inn just down the road. They have ice machines."

But all this rigorous penny pinching ignores the larger issue at hand.

It's as if the crew of the Titanic called all hands on deck to fix an overflowing toilet while the hull of the ship was being torn apart by a razor-sharp iceberg the size of Delaware.

The best time to save money isn't when a key grip is taking the lens cap off a 35mm camera. The best time to save money is when the executive committee cracks open a new box of marker pens to discuss the strategy.

This is the elephantine money pit in the room.

If I've seen it once, I've seen it a thousand times. The lower level marketing team, the ones hoping to become higher level marketing execs, decide the strategy should be one way:

"The car is more innovative…"

"The beer has fewer calories…"

"The flick flacks have better confabulation…"

And then the agency will dutifully chase that direction, sinking thousands of man hours into the effort. Including weekends, late nights and forgotten wedding anniversaries that will send many a teetering couple directly into the greedy hands of a divorce lawyer.

When the decks are printed, tweaked and reprinted, about 100 times, they will be presented to the next level up. Where, higher level marketing executives, also eager to climb the corporate ladder, will exert their power, pee all over the previous round of work and declare:

"The car is more fuel efficient..."

"The beer tastes better..."

"The flick flacks are plated with titanium for better confibulation..."

Sending the ad agency and their marketing partners back to the drawing board to do it all over again.
And again.
And again.

Sure you can eliminate the craft service smoothie drinks or stick your employees at the back of the plane across the aisle from the broken potty that has spitting blue water into the air since takeoff in Detroit.

But the people wasting the most money are not the worker bees. The folks frittering away the greenbacks like some coked-up Pentagon purchasing agents are the ones at the top of the org charts. And their indecision, mismanagement and myopic fear is costing billions of dollars, not millions.

Of course that's just the wasted money we can easily identify.

What about the incalculable costs generated by the children of overworked and under-reimbursed art directors and copywriters who, in the very near future, will be sitting with high-priced therapists and wondering why their mommies and daddies are not in any of the birthday party pictures.

We Need More Writers

Coming from someone who is keenly aware of the competition and how a glut of writers threaten to take food off my table, send me to a premature retirement and will one day land me behind the wheel of my Lexus, Ubering Angelenos to LAX, you might find it strange that I wish more people would write, but I do.

Keep in mind, I'm not saying we need more copywriters. Hell no, we need fewer of those.

But we do need more people familiar with the notion of structure, composition and disciplined thinking.

You see, with the advent of the computer, the internet and the god-awful open office plan, we have lost something vital to the future – the ability to express a thought with any degree of clarity. Speaking from experience, I know this to be true in the corporate world, but I suspect it applies elsewhere.

Today, we live in an age of abbreviated thinking. Texts, with no vowels. Decks, with bullet points but no insight. And last, but hardly least meaningful, mood boards.

Let's not forget about the rise of the emoji. If the emoji is any indication of where American business is going, it won't be long before we're grunting at each other and drawing on cave walls like our ancestors.

I know you think I'm exaggerating but I'm not.

Recently overheard, an account management type person offering up a thought starter to a creative type person:

"Hey Bill, I was thinking about that project. What about flanges?"

"What? What about them?"

"I don't know, I was just thinking about flanges."

End scene.

That's not the way it used to be.

From my days in the mailroom I remember a little something called the Interoffice Memo.

If a junior executive wanted to spring an idea on his or her cohorts, that junior executive took the time and the *effort* to spell it all out, from beginning to end, with a premise, logical proof points and a rock-solid conclusion that left no doubt this junior executive was upper management material.

Granted this was born out of a Cover Your Ass mentality, but at least it forced people to think and properly write out their ideas. Moreover, it produced a sense of accountability.

The world moves a lot faster since those days I pushed that damn mailroom cart up and down the hallways at Needham, Harper & Steers for $800 a month. But maybe we would all be doing ourselves a favor if we just slowed down.

When I was staff creative director, a young team was presenting their ideas for a new campaign. As they papered the wall in my office with colored Post It Notes, the art director qualified the pitch...

"I just want to say these ideas aren't fully baked yet but I think we're onto something."

"Good," I told them, *"bring it back when they're fully baked."*

All Hail the Freelancer

Sometimes the grapevine bears some very interesting fruit.

For instance years ago, a friend of mine found himself in a resources meeting with many of the agency brass (in this case the emphasis is on ass.) A big new project was rearing its head and the powers that be were trying to determine staffing/freelance needs.

Being a good friend, he threw my name in the hat. To which one peter-principled, smarmy taskmaster replied...

"Oh no, we're not bringing in Siegel. Every time I see him all I hear is cash registers ringing." (meaning I'm expensive)

Really?

In compliance with RoundSeventeen's strict no names policy I'm not naming names (though there's nothing in the policy about dropping clever little hints.) Suffice to say this anonymous fellow is to advertising what Sarah Palin is to the world of nuanced diplomacy.

Not only was the comment stupid. It was wrong.

Look, I'm no soothsayer, but I think we can all agree the ad industry is changing. And I'm gonna go out on a self-serving limb –because let's face it that's what soothsaying is all about – and suggest the future and very survivability of our cherished business depends on the freelancer.

What would lead me to such a diagnosis? After all I'm not in *the diagnosis business*.

The current model of an ad agency with its long tables of bescarved, bepierced, and betattoed creatives is simply unsustainable. Particularly with the decline of AOR relationships and the advent of jump ball scenarios.

You see while it may be cost effective to fill the hallways of the creative department with newly minted college graduates, the truth is they're getting paid whether they're fecklessly guiding billion dollar brands or just working on their sniping skills in the latest version of *Call of Duty*.

Freelancers, on the other hand, hit the ground running. You start the meter, they start the work.

And yes they might cost more, but only to the untrained eye.

Because before an agency pulls the trigger and brings in the mercenaries they go to the trouble of getting the brief signed. They make sure the assignment is buttoned up. That there is consensus. That deliverables are agreed upon. Agencies will go out of their way to get the most value out of the money they're spending on freelancers by doing all the legwork in advance.

In other words, they -- advertising agencies -- are operating at their most efficient.

Moreover, this has a push-pull effect on the clients. They're the ones footing the bill. So guess what happens? Clients start getting their shit together. They streamline approval processes. Clarify their thinking. And banish from the room anyone saying the following...

"I don't know why I don't like it, I just don't."

In other other words, they too are operating at their most efficient.

It's a win-win situation.

And that's just the tip of the proverbial iceberg. If this were a 273 page Powerpoint deck we would only be at page 6. Other advantages to bringing in the hired guns?

No healthcare costs. No melodrama. No paid vacations. Hell, you don't even need to feed the freelancers.

The money saved from buying bagels alone would finance Martin Sorrell's next yacht.

So you see unctuous unnamed "creative" executive who shall remain unnamed, you shouldn't shy away from hiring me or any other freelancer.

You should *pat* us on the back and *kneel* down and say, "*O*'my, thank you for being here."

Premature Exhibition

A week from today, the country will be talking about the Big Super Bowl.

And in my sad circle, friends and colleagues will be talking about the Big Super Bowl TV spots.

Not to crush anybody's spirit, but we'll be the only ones talking about the advertising come next Monday. Our collective naval-gazing has reached epic proportions. And make no mistake, I'm as guilty, if not guiltier, than most.

Of course some smart advertisers are not waiting a week. They'd like you to start forgetting about their marketing extravaganza right this second.

They've labored months, sacrificed weekends and played countless games of Scrabble or Candy Crush during production status meetings, why waste all that human capital on one showing during a football game everyone is too drunk to remember?

So, they've pre-released their spots.

And shot their wad before the big game.

It's better, they'll argue, because all the non-existent buzz they've deluded themselves into believing, can begin earlier. People will have an opportunity to view their content more often. And, and this is a big deal, they can squeeze another extra 100 likes on the YouTube channel.

If only I had employed such dexterous logic during my dating days when "getting out to an early start" was not embraced with such enthusiasm.

Call me Old School, but this grizzled 44 year old isn't buying it.

The idea of the Super Bowl spot is to reach through the flat screen TV, stop people in the middle of their Tostitos snack-sharing community moments™, and crack open their heads with 60 seconds of razzle dazzle that will have fans saying:

"That was fucking great. Why can't they make movies as good as they make the commercials?"

For those of you too young to remember, that's the way it was when Apple's *1984* spot first aired.

Or Monster.com's *"When I Grow Up".*

Or Miller Lite's *"Evil Beaver."*

And even more recently, Dodge's *"God Made a Farmer."*

But now, in the service of social media and the chase for Likes and Retweets, we've taken the element of surprise out of the hands of skilled art directors and crafty copywriters. It went right in the dustbin.

And sits next to long copy, wit, and intelligence; tools that are no longer useful in today's world of advertising.

If there's any buzz going on this week it's being generated by way-too-eager young media people gathered round their supervisor's cubicle…

"Hit the refresh button, see if we reached 1500 views yet."

Messing with Texas

Typically, at this point in the year, I'd be gearing up and foaming at the mouth for the opportunity to skewer the corporate-sponsored, digital jizz-a-palluzza, aka the yearly SXSW Festival.

Or as I like to refer to it, Burning Cash Man.

There's plenty of low hanging fruit here.

Hipsters, douchebags and impossibly prescient prophets, with one word names like Dingy, Melon, and Pazz, telling us what the industry will look like in five years.

I'd love to revisit their previous lectures from 2011 and see how many of their precious five year predictions came to fruition.

Because here's the thing, the shitty banner ads, rich media flash thingamajigs and obnoxious page takeovers that we all hated or ignored in 2011, are just as shitty, and indeed shittier, in 2016.

And the brand conversations we were supposed to be having with Wheat Thins, Right Guard Deodorant or even Pearl Vision, makers of fine reading glasses since 1947, we're still not having.

Perhaps that breakthrough brand engagement unit is just around the corner.

One can only hope.

Or at the very least waste countless hours at the many forums and panels at SXSW that will be discussing these riveting issues, just as they have been since they corrupted this indie music event 19 years ago.

If I were to hop on a plane and go to Austin, I wouldn't want to miss these seminal get togethers:

Maximizing your brand's inner potential, presented by Plaxo, Foursquare and Google+. *Tuesday 9:30 AM Presidential Suite at the Austin Ramada*

Elf Me 14, the Return of America's favorite photo upload phenomena. *Wednesday, 10:00 AM at The Austin Comfort Inn Wedding Banquet Room*

Going Long, a discussion with the industry's remaining three 45-year old copywriters. *Thursday, 6:00 AM at the Austin CVS*

Of course I have no plans to go to Austin. I was just there two months ago. And I loved the city.

But if I were to go, my itinerary would look a lot different.

For me, the most important must see events would include a return visit to Black's BBQ to feast on their pork shoulder slathered in super spicy homemade hot sauce.

Then I'd sample the legendary beef ribs at Langfords. And without fail make an obligatory stop at Franklin's where I'd hope to taste their classic slow-cooked Texas brisket.

If you didn't know, the line at Franklin's can stretch out a 1/4 mile long and diners have waited up to 5 hours in the pouring rain just to get in.

Imagine what their business would be like if they had a TweetDeck and a few good banner ads.

No Cannes Do

MEMO TO THE STAFF AT RICH SIEGEL WORLDWIDE

Date: 5/31/13

Re: Cannes

Subject: Cannes't

As many of you know the annual advertising festival celebrating the best and brightest the industry has to offer will soon be upon us.

There will be freshly-pressed linen.

There will be oysters, snails and other hard-to-look at snotty bottom feeders.

And there will be much revelry for the world-changing ideas trotted out onstage to an adoring crowd of deluded advertising narcissists who dare to refer to themselves as rock stars.

As many of you have also heard the sagging economy and the growing demand to meet shareholder expectations have forced many holding companies, and by proxy, their ad agencies, to cut unnecessary expenses and contract their staffing.

In light of these painful measures and in the desire to keep everyone here at Rich Siegel Worldwide gainfully employed, we have decided to suspend this year's gluttonous trip to southern France.

Before the groaning starts let's stop and consider the consequences.

Sure, it would be nice to soak up the sunshine at Les Rochers while nibbling on stinky cheese and sipping on a $500 bottle of *Louis Roederer*, but it would leave an awful aftertaste knowing that it came at the expense of someone's mortgage and/or tuition payment.

Sure, it would be fun to turn up the collars on our polo shirts, don a Trilby hat and hang out at the Gutter Bar drinking 100-year old single malt whiskey while puffing on a *Don Arturo Edicion Aniversario*, but it would also be a little tone deaf knowing the account coordinator, who worked so tirelessly this past year, is now slinging and singing at the local Cold Stone Creamery.

And yes, it would be great to pal around with a bunch of hard-drinking, hard-body Brazilians who've made a career out of flashy spec ads for condoms, bubble gum and novelty socks, but have never faced the daunting challenge of a bank ad or a year end dealer sales event.

However, the pain of pink slipping so many good decent people makes all that, impossible.

We here at Rich Siegel Worldwide want to go to Cannes in

the worst possible way.

But out of respect, prudence, and just plain common sense, we also recognize that going to Cannes would be the worst possible decision.

If I were King of the Forest

Like everybody else in the country, I filed my tax returns last week. Unlike most people in the country however, I file as a freelancer.

Technically, I'm self-employed and the owner of my own company, a fictional organization called Rich Siegel Worldwide.

The truth is I very rarely do direct-to-client work and mostly serve as a hired gun to many different ad agencies. The other truth is I will never be the owner or sole proprietor or even CEO of my own company.

There are many reasons for that, principally because I'm not very adept at schmoozing clients. Nor am I able to work up a shit-eating grin when they make bonehead remarks.

These are my flaws and demons and I have come to accept them.

Nevertheless, on occasion, I will picture myself as the man at the top of some imaginary org chart and wonder how I would do things differently at my ad agency. In other words, I wonder what it would say in my company handbook.

Rule #1. At the end of every year, every employee gets a raise and a bonus. It doesn't have to be equal, it just has to be fair. It's a little something called incentive. Without it an agency cannot move forward. If we can't afford a raise and a bonus for everyone, then no one gets one. Including me.

Rule #2. The doors open at 9:00 AM and they close at 7:30 PM. And they stay closed on the weekends. That's a little more than 50 hours a week. Nobody should spend more than 50 hours a week thinking about advertising. Employees who have balanced lives also have better ideas. And better attitudes. And most importantly, better feelings towards me.

Rule #3. If we pitch a piece a business and we win, everybody gets a taste. If you'll excuse the simplistic baseball analogy. When the Yankees win a pennant or a divisional championship or even a World Series, they don't gallop into a locker room and hand out Dom Perignon to Jeter, Petite and Cano, or just those who batted in some key RBI's. They roll out the Korbel and everybody partakes. That's what winning new business is about. There is no "Fuck you, you didn't work on the pitch" in TEAM.

Rule #4. Once a month there will be Mailroom Clerk Appreciation Day. Inside every mailroom clerk there is a CEO just waiting to blossom. I'm not saying that just because I was a former mailroom clerk. OK, yes I am. But let's face it, they, and lowly account coordinators, and executive assistants, are the people who do the heavy lifting of an ad agency. And in fact, most organizations. Their work is rarely recognized. But it should be, because these are the people, not some hot-snot Art Center graduate with a stingy-brim Fedora, who will rise through the ranks and be in a position to return the love someday.

Rule #5. No smelly people. If you smoke excessively or have halitosis or do not bathe regularly, you can expect a visit from HR. We will tolerate all manner of eccentric behavior at Rich Siegel Worldwide, but if you smell like a baby needing a diaper change you will be sent home. And eventually replaced by someone who has the good sense not to offend my oversized nose.

I'm sure there are 100 more rules I could commit to paper but I suspect if I pursue this any further I will just be providing more evidence of my business naiveté. No organization, particularly an ad agency, could live up to these ideals.

But if an agency were to subscribe to an owner's manual like this, or even give lip service to it, they'd never have to spend another dime for recruitment.

Take Your Job and Shove It

I'm coming up on 13 years as a freelancer.

It's the longest time I've ever held a particular job title.
Previous to that, I had spent 6 years working at Chiat/Day.
But I'm pretty sure my last year I was phoning it in and
spending inordinate amounts of time on monster.com, or
dozens of other job boards.

Lately, perhaps due to the seismic changes in the Los Angeles
advertising community, I've been asked how I handle life
as a freelancer. Which is often followed by,

*"Don't you ever want to go back on staff? You know, for the
job security?"*

If I did go back on staff it would not be for the "job security."

It would be for the direct deposit checks. Or the paid
dental cleaning. Or the opportunity to spend 12 hours a
day with stunning 25-year old women who say charming
things like, *"Oh you're so funny. Just like my Dad."*

You see "job security" is an illusion. It's a Unicorn. It's
Sasquatch. It's The Ark of the Covenant. It's a Donald Trump
Thought Filter.

These are things that simply do not exist.

Job security does not exist because fairness does not exist.
Fairness does not exist because meritocracy does not exist.

And meritocracy does not exist because Careerism, with a capital C, does exist.

I'll give you a good example.

A friend of mine was in charge of the creative department for a certain client at a certain unnamed Orange County agency. Prior to taking that job he had been a successful freelancer, but decided he wanted something more "permanent." So he re-entered agency life and poured himself into the work. Sales went up. Month after month after month. Then his client hired a new CMO.

The new CMO also wanted job security. So she did what all new CMO's do: disregard any success of the past, clean house and install her own people. And before you could say, "two years of aggregated growth and sales expansion", my buddy, who sat through countless meetings, who bit his tongue at numerous stupid criticisms, and who fought off every instinct to throttle the numbnuts across the table, was shown the door.

A glutton for punishment, a year later he tried his hand at a different agency hoping for a different result. The circumstances changed, the outcome did not. Or as a brilliant account executive once explained to me:

"Same shit, different shithouse."

These stories, or permutations of them, happen here in Southern California, in SF, in Chicago, and all over NY.

And, they will continue happening. Which might have bothered me in the past but doesn't bother me now.

Because I have job security. Albeit, a not-so-conventional definition.

My job security comes from within.

It comes from knowing that I am my best resource. That I over-deliver on every opportunity. And that I control my own fate.

Of course it's not all internal. My job security also stems from the quality of work in today's advertising environment.

Did you see the commercials during this year's Super Bowl?

Excuse Me?

I've been in advertising many, many years.

I know dozens of my contemporaries are looking for ways to get out. These are mostly staffers, working managerial positions and not having half the fun they used to. Not that ad agencies haven't tried to bring back the fun.

Ping Pong tables.
Foosball apparatus.
Pop-A-Shot machines.

You'd think you had walked into a Dave & Busters, not an advertising agency.

It hasn't worked and most agency people are desperately looking for the exit door.

I'm not looking for a way out, mostly because I like working the way I do. As a mercenary. Sometimes actually going in to an office. Sometimes working from my house. But rarely meeting with planners, account people or clients. Or dealing with any of the *mishigas* that can instigate the fight or flight response.

In that respect, I'd like to work many, many more years in this crazy business.

Not to get a spot in the Super Bowl or create another award

winning campaign, though that would be nice.

Not to build my portfolio. I've given up on that.

Not even to prove the remarkably obvious point that age and experience are more instrumental to an agency's success than free bagels, Friday afternoon keg parties or a creative department full of clueless hipsters in dime store douchy hats.

No. I'd like to work in advertising so that one day, maybe, perhaps, with a little luck, on the off chance, with a sprinkle of serendipity, I might just once hear a client say something intelligent, for example:

"I like the dog, but wouldn't it be funnier with a monkey?"

"I have a gut feeling about this, let's skip the focus groups."

"This feels likes spoon feeding, we shouldn't talk down to our consumers."

"I know this should have a social media component, but let's save that money and sink it into the production budget."

"Can we give this more white space?"

"I like it. I don't care what my boss thinks."

"Now that the planner has left the room, can you tell me what he does?"

I could probably come up with 100 more of the quips, but the codeine-based cough medicine I've been taking is making me sleepy.

Mad Stacks, Yo.

Want to make a ton of cash and be the darling of the corporate world?

Write a book or an article about why employees don't want anything tangible, money for instance, and would prefer soft compensation, like greater freedom or room for personal "growth."

Last week, *Inc.* magazine published a piece by corporate apologist Geoffrey James entitled, "10 Things Employees Want More than A Raise." I'm sure the article was clipped by HR professionals throughout the land.

Mr. James is a standing member of the Society of American Business Editors and has had work published in the *NY Times*, so I don't want to be disrespectful.

But, FUCK YOU, Geoffrey James!

You could have used a good editor before *Inc.* ran your recent article.

Because, let's be honest, there aren't 10 Things Employees Want More Than A Raise.

There aren't 5 Things.

There aren't 3 Things.

In fact, and I'm speaking anecdotally and on behalf of ALL labor, there isn't ANY thing employees want more than a raise.

What he, and corporate anthropologists of his ilk, fail to understand is we go to work to get paid.

We don't put on starched clothing, sit on the 405 freeway and give up 10 hours of our daily 24 because we want to. We do it for the money. So that we have food, clothing and shelter. And with a little luck, enough entertainment to make us forget all the mismanagement, office politics and corporate bullshit we're forced to endure.

We're not interested in company pride. Or free bagels. Or false camaraderie or respect.

We want money. And we want more of it.

How do I know this is true? There's a softball question. Put the wingtip shoe on the other foot.

Imagine a C-suite executive coming up for his or her performance review and being told, *"We're not giving out raises or bonuses this year. But we can offer you a wide selection of morale-building T-shirts. Or, if you'd like to take some adult education classes at the Learning Annex, the company will be happy to pay for it."*

Here's the other thing. Companies and HR people who buy into this line of horse hockey aren't doing themselves any favors.

You see, in the real world, the world of free market practices, companies that pay well, attract better talent. Better talent makes a better product or delivers a better service. Companies that put out better quality, make better profits.

I may not have an MBA or even a sophisticated knowledge of management, but you show me a company that doesn't give out raises and I'll show you a labor pool of disgruntled employees feverishly working the linkedin connections.

And going home at night with as many Post-It Notes and leather moleskin notepads as they can stuff in their backpacks.

The Fenske Credo

I've made no secret of my admiration for Mark Fenske.

Mark is a professor at VCU now, but when he made a living as a copywriter he wrote unlike any other. Perhaps that's why his name was all over the awards books, which made it a whole lot easier to mimic his style.

In addition to teaching, Mark maintains – and I use that word sparingly – a blog. He puts up an entry every month or so, which means he has about two regular readers, me and whenever he does an infrequent spellcheck.

His most recent entry however struck a chord.

He told his students, aspiring copywriters and art directors:

"Just do the opposite of everything you see."

His reasoning is simple. 99% of everything you see on TV, Twitter, Facebook, etc. is utter crap. That is undeniable. If you want to do something good, don't do crap.

It is for me, the first litmus test of any work I present.

If it sounds like, looks like, or smells like anything that's already out there I don't want to have any part of it.

If only clients bought into the same criteria. They don't.

Their rationale is equally simple. If it doesn't sound or look or smell like anything out there, they get nervous.

Because it's different. And, if a campaign dares to be different it also, by definition, flirts with failure.

And as much as corporate yahoos and motivational masturbators would have us believe in the redemptive power of failure, the truth is Chief Marketing Officers with multiple mortgages and a sweet corner office, will run away from risk faster than Republicans will run away from anything that sounds like sensible gun laws.

As a result we get shit, shitty and shittier work.

Digital scavenger hunts. Overwrought manifestos. Or happy smiling millennials in contrived situations speaking committee-written adtalk to other happy smiley millennials whose manicured beards should be pulled out by hand and shoved down their precious organic-only pie holes.

And everything has to be Big. Big effects. Big music. Big scenarios.

Sadly, it's also why there's little chance we'll see work that's truly authentic, insightful and delightfully human.

I'm sure Fenske would agree, God blessed the Creative Director who has the balls to ask for small.

Bring Me the Head of Charles Schwab

Last week I visited the offices of Charles Schwab, where under great duress, I had to divulge a lifetime of all my financial mishaps. While it was painful it was also therapeutic. A way to get my financial house in order and rid myself of the investment demons that have haunted me for years.

We all have inner demons.

Perhaps those of us in the ad industry have slightly more than others. We pour ourselves into our work, and day after day that work is rejected. Or Frankensteined. Or picked apart by a former frat boy, who now has a degree in advertising and a junior position with a client but doesn't have a clue as to the contributions of Gossage, Bernbach or Jay Chiat.

It takes a thick skin to work as a creative in advertising. It takes an even thicker skin to look back at the file of all the great ideas that never got produced. That file seems to grow exponentially.

Here's where these two paths – Charles Schwab and years of unproduced work – collide.

A long, long time ago, we, TBWA/Chiat/Day, were asked to pitch the Charles Schwab account. I love pitching new business. It's one of the rare opportunities to hit an unmitigated home run.

You start with nothing, no client mandates, no past

faux pas, no limitations. And if you win, you come away with new billings, new opportunities, new ways to start losing the business.

One of the writers on our team was Mike Collado. He and his partner had come up with a breakthrough campaign that I will in no way do any justice. Sadly this brilliant campaign never made it past the front door and the good folks at Schwab never had the opportunity to see it.

But thanks to the self destructive career path I have embarked on, you will. Here's the idea in a nutshell:

While driving himself home from a three day intensive industry conference, Mr. Schwab falls asleep at the wheel. His car careens off a cliff. And he is decapitated, that's right decapitated. Miraculously, the head of Charles Schwab, the vessel of all that financial wisdom, survives.

A young couple in a pick up truck stops to investigate the carnage. They find the head of Charles Schwab, rescue him and nurse him back to health with ice and lots of aspirin.

In return, he schools them on the advantages of a diversified portfolio with a balanced mix of asset allocation. They prosper and have the wherewithal to send their three children off to private colleges.

The story doesn't end there. In subsequent commercials, the head of Charles Schwab travels this great nation, dispensing valuable and actionable financial advice to all those who will listen to this disembodied guru. I don't recall the narrative gymnastics of how the head got from place to place. But it did. And anyone who had it, had the means to secure financial independence.

It was the classic 'talking head' campaign.
And this one, if you'll pardon the pun, had legs.

Sadly, we'll never know if this would have succeeded or not. But riddle me this, can you tell me about the last Charles Schwab commercial you saw?

I'm betting you can't.

The tagline they currently use is, Talk to Chuck. And in essence it's the same strategy, get great advice by talking with Charles Schwab. But it's sleepy and it doesn't have anything memorable, like a decapitation.

And that's the fundamental problem with today's advertising, not enough decapitations.

Man O'Manifesto

It has now been more than 8 months since I wrote my last manifesto.

And I do believe we are entering a new era of advertising.

An era I am calling The Age of the Antifesto.

I for one couldn't be happier.
People hate the manifesto. And that's fine with me, because I hate writing them.

There was a time I was being brought in to agencies to crank out two manifestos in a week. That became three. And then the three manifestos a week quickly became three manifestos in three days. Three days quickly became one day.

And on one occasion I had a client ask me for a new manifesto in 45 minutes!

Was it any good?

Good is in the eye of the beholder.
 It assumes a standard.
A standard that…

See how easy it is to slip into that crappy pseudo-important tone of voice?

When manifestos had their heyday, back in the 90's, I had the good fortune to be working with Mark Fenske, who was, and is, a writer's writer. Mark is a naturally-built middle linebacker, standing 6'4" and weighing in at a very decent bowler's score.

As such, he manhandles words as if they were a skinny punter from the Czech Republic.

I still have some of Mark's old manifestos in my files. And refer to them when the going gets tough. Or steal from them when the deadline gets impossible.

In any case the pendulum is swinging back the other way.

Not every company can be like Apple. Nor should they be. Computers impact people lives. Unscented deodorants, restaurant-style tortilla chips, online hotel aggregators, do not.

Smart CEO's who want to sell their shit are contacting ad agencies to help them sell more of their shit. And they're doing so without the aid of some hastily-written, easily-ignored corporate poetry.

Yet, weeks from now, sure as automotive deals that won't last forever, I will be asked to write some aspirational horse manure for some delusional CMO who believes his company's doohickey or whatchamacallit can rescue mankind.

Ignoring the most common of common sense.

Because the Soda Pop Pushers, Mayonnaise Makers and Fast Food Vendors who are crazy enough to think they can change the world, are most definitely the ones who cannot.

No Mood for Mood Boards

If you haven't guessed I am a man of many pet peeves.

You don't get to my age without having acquired some irritations. Or in my case, way too many.

Perhaps I should learn to meditate but I can't help thinking nothing will dry the well faster than a sense of tranquility and ease with the world at large.

And so I willfully remain peeved. And the world returns the favor with an endless supply of asininity.

Nothing illustrates that more than the ad agency mood board.

Years ago, my partner and I were working at a shop, an unnamed local satellite of a much larger worldwide agency. The creative directors in charge were young. Given to tattoos, Capri pants and artisanal coffee; all well-documented pet peeves of mine.

While they were long on affectations, they were noticeably shorthanded in their ability to tell a story.

And so we found ourselves, on several late nights, preparing elaborate mood boards to accompany and elucidate our scripts.

My best thinking and my best writing are done early so I'm

not fond of being in the office at 8 o'clock on any night. By then Final Jeopardy has been answered and I've been robbed of an opportunity to flaunt my abundant trivial knowledge in front of my family.

I'm particularly foul about staying late to do a Google image search for just the right rustic farmhouse barn.

Or the perfectly coiffed middle-aged housewife.

Or the demographically-correct breed of pet dog.

Let's say you're a client, you're the Chief Marketing Officer of a large multibillion dollar company. You've spent years in the business and have an intuitive feel for how a brand's message needs to be conveyed.

And let's say I'm in your fancy Chief Marketing Officer's office and I'm presenting you a script. And just for example the spot opens with, "a woman walks into a luxurious high end apartment."

Do you really need to see a mood board in order to under-stand the visual cues one might find in a luxurious high end apartment?

No.

If anything you should be insulted that we, the ad agency, have discounted your imagination and opted to spoon feed you meaningless generic images screen grabbed off a computer while eating crappy, over-spiced Thai food.

You should rightfully be insulted and cheesed off that we assigned billable hours to that stupid endeavor.

Conversely, if you are a CMO and you need a mood board because you can't conjure up the images in your head, well, then I would respectfully submit that your reach has far exceeded your grasp.

Mergers and Supplications

You might remember not long ago we heard of the proposed $35 billion merger of Omnicom (an alma mater) and Publicis (also an alma mater.)

This "marriage of equals" was to bring us "untold synergy and a global platform with which to ideate, implement and execute scalable innovative and disruptive communications devices for the betterment of our clients and indeed all of mankind."

Which is another way of saying a few obscenely rich white dudes could have expanded their harem of mistresses and purchased a new fleet of yachts.

In today's modern advertising industry there's not even the illusion of fairness.

Worker bees like myself, and probably you, never get equity in an ad agency, particularly those owned by the holding companies. You and I were not invited to the wealth distribution party. You have to be a made man or a made woman – oh who are we kidding it's only men, white men – to secure a position at the billion dollar feeding trough.

And getting to the top of Mt. Advertising is not a matter of creating great ideas, entering the iconic language of pop culture or even mastering this new digital landscape.

If I'm not mistaken, the Capos...er, CEO's of the four holding companies, Messrs. Wren, Levy, Sorrell and Nadal have
never written a headline.

Never comped a layout.
Never scratched out a banner ad in their life.
I'd bet a testicle not one of them has ever laid hands on a
gator board.

All that is moot.

Because the urge to merge lost its surge. The deal was called
off. There was some hooey in the press about the marriage
failing because of a "clash of cultures."

Give me a break. Holding companies don't have cultures.
Holding companies have vaults where they hold all the
money. Maybe the Omnicom vault was jet black and the
Publicis vault was charcoal grey. A junior art director with a
Pantone chart could have mediated that little clash.

Adweek reported that both companies spent a combined
$100 million in fees for lawyers and international accountants
to sort out the deal; the deal that didn't happen. And all it
bought them was a public relations nightmare.

That money has literally been pissed into the wind.

How could it have been better spent?

* $100 million could have been set aside for a pension plan,

you know for the advertising people who actually do the advertising work for an advertising company.

* $100 million could have been used to build proper offices. Not some SuperDesk™, but real offices, with doors that close. So that you can get on the phone with your doctor and describe in detail that funny rash you discovered on your inner thigh.

* $100 million could have been used for flight upgrades. Comfortable, humane seats in business class for demoralized copywriters who have been asked to give up time with their friends and family and don't want to sit 7 hours in coach, in a middle seat wedged between a fat guy and an older woman who chain smokes and wears too much perfume.

* $100 million could have been spread across the board. Divied up between the collective 130,000 employees at both organizations. I did the math. It works out to a $750 bonus for each and every employee.

Imagine the memo some smart CEO could have penned to accompany that unexpected windfall:

Dear Omnicom or Publicis employee,

We've recently been approached to merge with one of our competitors. This is because of the value and worth you have given our company. Your loyalty, determination and hard work have raised our profile in the industry.

None of this would have happened had it not been for you.

After careful consideration of the deal and before we engage a horde of outrageously expensive lawyers, we have turned down that offer. Mostly because we're not in the merger and acquisition business.

We're in the business of advertising. And our most valuable assets ride up and down the elevator everyday.

Accordingly, we'd like you to have this small token of our appreciation – a check for $750.

Pay some bills, go out to dinner, throw a party for your son to make up for the birthday you missed.

And thank you for making us look good.

Signed,

Your Leader

Of course, it didn't happen that way.

It never does.

Too Many Freelancers

In the past week and a half I have discovered three colleagues who decided to hand in their staffer key cards, with all its incumbent amenities: 24 hour access to the office, free weekend parking and enough complimentary NutraSweet packets, colored Post-It Notes and mechanical pencils to last a lifetime.

Not surprisingly, they've jumped right into the Freelance Pool.

My friend Mike, who bills himself as the World's Best Freelancer (er….cough) often complains that my nonstop railing against the holding companies and my deadly accurate portrayal of sad agency life is only fueling the creative department departures and the current glut.

"Siegel, what are you doing? You sit there in your pajamas, drink your coffee, put on your noise-canceling headphones in your comfortable den and drone on about Open Office Plans and shitty status meetings, all while pulling down a healthy day rate. And sometimes two. You're a Retention Manager's nightmare."

In deference to Mike, and other well established freelancers who now find themselves swarmed by competition and fighting harder and harder for gigs, I've decided to spill some ugly truths about the freelance life.

Dry Spells – Contrary to what some believe, there are

times when my phone doesn't ring and the only email I get is from pharmaceutical companies pitching me their expensive, hard-to-swallow penis enhancement pills.

When one gig ends I don't seamlessly roll right into the next. I'll often find myself in a non-revenue earning gap of a day or two. Or even three. It's difficult to know what to do with myself. There's only so much napping and daytime bourbon-drinking an underachieving writer can do.

Smiling and Dialing – Something else they don't tell you when you leave the safety net of the agency, you have to hustle. You are in pitch mode every day. You may be a 44 year old copywriter with more than 30 years experience, but that wealth of experience means little, if anything, to the folks in charge of handing out the gigs. Moreover, they're getting younger and younger and may not even be familiar with your dated credentials.

"What's a double page spread? Are you sure you have the right number?"

Making Nice – In my early days, I was quite the hothead. My anger would get the best of me. I would snap. Bark. And bite. I did not suffer fools well. I still don't. But now, as a freelancer, a temporary employee whose livelihood depends on being collegial, when a client says or requests something stupid, I feel compelled to bite my tongue and reply with words that do not come naturally to me: "Awesome", "Super" and "Wish I had thought of that."

Trust me, that can be the hardest part about being a freelancer.

Really hard.

Think long on this my art director or copywriter friend. You may not be cut out for a life with a lot less stress, a lot more money and unpredictable flexibility in your schedule.

In which case, I suggest you keep your day job.

"But He's Not A Digital Copywriter."

Being inside an ad agency gives me great joy.

On occasion.

For instance, I love going to work at a place of business with people dressed for the business of slacking off. The number of Oxford shirts and well-pressed pants in my closet is dwarfed by the number of T-Shirts, cargo shorts and well-worn flip flops.

I love the freedom of an ad agency.

There isn't a day that goes by when I'm not summoned to a desk or cubicle to see the latest video that's eating up the internet – yes, I do want to see a snake swallow a porcupine. Hell, I'll wait around to see what happens at the other end.

And of course, I love the free food.

It's literally a cavalcade of bagels, donuts and chocolate chip scones, brought in by fawning reps hoping to secure some business for their photographers, music composers and illustrators.

I like to look at the food but never sample it.

I also like watching the young people scarf it down, oblivious to the fact that their slowing metabolisms will soon change their swipe-ability on Tinder.

But there is nothing that makes me happier than coming up with a solve, particularly a digital solve.

Last week for instance, and without revealing any agency or client details, my partner and I were asked to jump in on a digital assignment. We are both painfully aware that we are considered creative department dinosaurs. And that younger creatives are drooling with anticipation, waiting for the old dudes to lay something on the table that has something to do with Morse Code or old wooden butter churners.

But that didn't happen.

In less than 36 hours – the new time allotment given on any ad agency project – we turned around a number of noteworthy solutions. No sooner did they pass from our hands to the Creative Director, who excitedly looped in the Chief Creative Officer, who singled out one of our ideas, and declared the concept, "fucking great."

Not bad for a couple of old farts who can correctly identify Howard Gossage, Helmut Krone and George Lois.

Time will tell whether the idea moves forward or comes to fruition. To be honest, none of that matters.

To me, the fun part of the business is doing what many people assume I can no longer do.

I'm not all up in your face with HTML coding, pushing content up the revenue stream or designing an engagement unit that holistically leverages the core brand essence across various static and mobile consumer touch points.

Hell, I don't even know what I just wrote.

But if you need an idea, a real idea, and not some drivel from a PBR-drinking, empty headed poser sporting dreads and $500 ripped jeans from Japan, you know where to reach me.

A Trip to the Abusement Park

If I had a second shot at my life in advertising, I probably would have done a few things different.

One of my regrets is that I never became an Executive Creative Director or a Chief Creative Officer. I know I would have liked the opportunity to helm all the creative decisions and leave my own imprint on the business. I like to naively think that no "shit" would have made it out the door.

But that day will never happen as I have become a victim of my own hard-headedness and my self-evident tendency towards bloviation.

Instead of speaking my mind, I should have, as Lee Clow once told me, learned the art of listening. In fact, if you were to question Lee, he would tell you that his success stems from the ability to listen.

It's that simple.

In short, there are no second shots.

And now, at 44, you could argue that my career record needle is fast approaching the paper label in the center of the album. That has its own benefits.

For instance, I can speak freely on unpleasant events and unpleasant people (without names of course) with little or no fear of retribution.

About twenty years ago, my partner and I were asked to head up the pitch for the new Universal Studios Islands of Adventure Amusement Park in Orlando. The business was worth $100 million and the agency was willing to jump through hoops to please the pitch consultant, a monumentally noxious man who made a habit of talking with his mouth full.

He insisted any agency team working on this huge piece of business have a first hand view of the park. Not unreasonable. Except at the time, the park had not been built yet. And it was August. And it was in Orlando. Orlando, Florida.

In other words, it was memorably hot.

For three days, in unbearable T-shirt soaking humidity, we walked around a 150 acre empty lot and looked at steel I-beams, scaffolding and empty pits. The torture punctuated by our over-zealous, mealy mouth host.

"Over here will be the Superman Roller Coaster, which will soar 450 feet onto the air and give riders an excellent view of the Hulk Roller Coaster which will be built in that pit, once they figure out the drainage situation."

Did I mention that the guided tour was often delivered while our host was scarfing down croissants, hot dogs, pizza, falafel and baba ganoush? This man had an insatiable appetite.

If I ate like him, I'd look like me.

When the useless walking tour of the construction site was over, we were treated to a 3 hour briefing. Making matters even worse, the agency we were pitching against was also in the large conference room. When we weren't sizing up the competition we had to listen to Marathon Man and his mammoth sized ego drone on about roller coasters.

At the conclusion, my partner John Shirley did one of the funniest things I had ever witnessed. He turned to the competing agency.

"If you're thinking about a campaign where people stand up in their seats and scream at the top of their lungs as the roller coaster free falls, don't. Because we already have that story boarded up."

Everyone laughed.

We were Chiat/Day and would never resort to such overworked hackneyed amusement park advertising.

The other agency had no such compunction.

They pitched an entire campaign of people riding coasters, waving their arms and screaming at the top of their lungs.

They won the business.

Why I Sucked at Being a Creative Director
Part II

Can you feel it?

It's coming.

The much-anticipated Christmas/New Year's break. Or
the period advertising people refer to as the most likely time
I will get home before 9 o'clock and not get called in to work
a weekend. Of course that can all change at the drop
of an RFP.

Or if Johnny Client decides, after months of painstaking
committee fucking, rewriting, tweaking, reshooting and
re-editing…

"I'm not sure our new Super Bowl spot feels fresh and Disruptive™
as it did when I first signed off on it. Can you guys show me
something new? On Dec. 26? Thanks."

The end of the year has also got me thinking. A moment
for introspection. That's when I thought I would follow up
on the most popular post ever written for RoundSeventeen
– Why I Sucked at Being a Creative Director.

People like reading about my many faults and shortcomings.
And they don't make any attempt to hide their glee. It's like
an inverted schadenfreude, which is usually savored in private. In fact when I published the original post, I had

"friends" offering to pile on.

"I'll tell you another reason you suck, Siegel."

Thanks, but no thanks. I can handle this assignment on my own.

Anyway, picking up where I left off. *(see page 13)*

7. **I have a short fuse.** There I said it. I won't take it back. And I won't go in search of any fuse-enhancement pills. Not only is my temper short, it's volatile. I do not suffer fools gladly. I can deal with people who are sneaky, political, brilliant, drunk, or perpetually drunk, but I have no stomach for people who are just plain stupid. And sadly when you've sat in three hour long wardrobe meetings discussing the merits of a cardigan vs. a vested sweater, you know there's plenty of stupid to go around.

Mind you, there have been many successful creative directors with short fuses, but they had redeeming qualities that I don't have, like wavy hair or nice shoes.

8. **There's no me in Team**. I know many people belong to the Congregation of Collaboration, I'm not one of them. There was a time, a better time, in advertising when I knew the names of all the great writers and art directors. I won't call them "rock stars" because I hate that delusional metaphor, but they were the heavily-awarded individuals who had made a name for themselves by standing out from the crowd. If you've seen the credit list on any work lately

you know credit nowadays belongs to the crowd. Assistant
Associate Coordinators never enjoyed such limelight.
In 2016, I didn't touch one assignment that wasn't also
manhandled by half the creative department.

9. **Lost my wind sock.** I can read a room and can generally
tell how and what to present. The industry, on the other
hand, is thoroughly confounding. I always assumed clients
want work that will make a splash, move the masses and
create a recognizable spike in sales. That tells me to plant a
flag, establish a unique tone of voice and execute it loudly on
TV, in print and outdoor. But the well-informed creative
director of today knows otherwise. As the Swedes on
Happyish were fond of saying, "It's not about campaigns
anymore." It's about getting Likes. Going viral. And to quote
myself from a previous post, creating a *"vast array of
Frivolous Fuckwadian Digital Knick Knacks™."*

10. **ADD.** In addition to my aforementioned short fuse, I
have the even more crippling affliction of a short attention
span. It's why it took me close to three years to write
*RoundSeventeen & 1/2, The Names have Been Changed to
Protect the Ineffcient* -- the book none of you bought. It's
why I can't see a screenplay through from beginning to end.
And it's why if a spot has reached the point of a 15th, 16th or
17th rewrite, I'll simply cave in and say, "have the client
write it and I'll just polish up the turd."

There you have it, my Top Ten reasons on why I sucked at being a creative director.

Could I write ten more? Of course I could. But then this thinly-veiled humblebrag would lose its disingenuous sheen of modesty.

Besides, it's getting a little long in the tooth and I just rummaged through the pantry and found some chocolate flavored Pop-Tarts with my name on it.

Let's go Panelling

I know my friends down in Austin, eating their artisanal corn beef hash and drinking their cold-filtered, kale-infused, Peruvian-roasted mocha lattes know what time it is. Do you?

It's SXSW time again.

This year promises to be bigger and better than ever. Even the Obamas are showing up, which will surely clog South Congress Ave. and give the residents something to buzz about other than the new shipment of alligator boots over at Allen's House of Fine Cowboy Wear.

Even as we speak, panels are being coalesced and presenters are nervously going over their material hoping to wow the young, ear-gauge-sporting adverati who have not yet been beaten into submission or yielded to the onset of industrial grade cynicism and bitterness.

Fortunately, as in years past, I have obtained a sneak preview of what's to come at SXSW, which I'm more than happy to share with you:

March 14, 9:00 AM - 10:00 AM – **FourSquare Introduces K9Square,** a new killer app that allows users to check in and tell the world where their dog is located. SXSW attendees will have the opportunity to witness this incredible new innovation, which FourSquare CEO Don Winkhood promises will be the first in its ever-expanding suite of digital knick knacks.

March 15, 2:00 PM - 3:00 PM – The efficiency folks from Sigma Six have returned with an encore presentation of: **How to Reinvent Customized Systems with Scalable Supply Chains.** followed by **Scaling Your Supply Chain to Meet the Needs of your Reinvented Customized System.**

March 18, 10:00 AM - 10:00 PM – **Increasing Corporate Nimbleosity**™. This mammoth 12 hour panel will redefine the operations Nimbleability™ at your ad agency. A holistic approach that demonstrates how all the constituents at your shop can not only have their voices heard, but play a meaningful and effective role in the delivery of your advertising vehicles. The panel will be followed by a question and answer period where remaining guests will talk in circles until 3:00 AM or until the housekeeping staff at the Ramada Inn arrives to clean the William Taft Conference Room.

March 19, Noon - 2:00 PM – **The SXSW Build Your Own Burrito Bar.** It's back and it's bigger than ever. Designed by the renowned architect who gave us the SuperDesk™, the Burrito Bar is one long 75 foot continuous table that spans the width of 6th Ave. It can accommodate hundreds of hungry ad professionals, whether they be creatives, account managers, UX designers, planning directors, regular planners, junior planners, planning strategists or associate assistant planners. Because let's face it, when it comes to burritos there can never be too many cooks in the kitchen.

March 23, 5:00 PM – **Closing Convocation** given by this year's special guest, Bob Hoffman – the Ad Contrarian. Attendee who correctly guesses how many times Bob says "Fuck", "Asshole" or "Digital Douchebag", will take home a brand new Buick Enclave.

That's right, a Buick.

Can't Get No Respect

I want to make an apology.

I don't know who I'm apologizing to, but I want to go on record with my contrition.

Allow me to explain.

I like to think I live by a certain code. I hold others up to a similar set of standards so it's only natural those standards apply to me. Otherwise, I could be accused of being the world's biggest asshole, a charge I am quite familiar with.

Part of that code is responding to email, phone calls or any other gestures for my attention.

And so, if I haven't gotten back to you, it isn't because I haven't tried. Maybe it fell through the cracks. Went to my junk folder. Or simply slipped my quickly degenerating mind. It certainly was not meant as a measure of disrespect.

But let's face it. We live in highly disrespectful times. And this shit has become endemic.

This is not a thinly-veiled missive towards anyone in particular, this is a double-barreled full blast of rock salt at the entire industry. And humanity in general.

Common courtesy has become singularly uncommon.

It takes all of 13 seconds to hit the reply button on an email, write "thank you but we're not interested" and click the mouse to send the minutest measure of collegial respect.

I know, I timed it.
But apparently that's too much.

I've been doing a lot of Smiling and Dialing lately in order to stay ahead of the freelance glut on the market. And I am flabbergasted by the soaring level of disrespect.

Last week a recruiter was looking for a Creative Director/ Freelance Copywriter for a juicy three month gig here in Los Angeles. Naturally, I inquired.

Shockingly, I was told I lacked the qualifications for the assignment. With the possible exception of feminine hygiene products or video gaming software, I like to think there's very little this 44 year old copywriter can't handle.

It wasn't the response I expected but at least it was a response. She was dead wrong in her assessment but at least she showed some measure of respect.

I wish that were true of agencies and clients who demand impossible turnarounds, lower day rates, extended hours and last minute requests to completely re-haul, re-tool and rebrand a Fortune 100 Global Company over the course of a weekend.

Is it too much to ask for a little professional respect?

And how 'bout getting some air conditioning up in this bitch?

Retainment vs. Recruitment

Eureka!

Woo-Hoo!

Yeeeeeessssssss!!!

You might be wondering what all the excitement is about.
Or, you might have turned your short attention span to
Adweek to read another one of their crack journalistic pieces:
27 under 27, The 27 Media Associates Under 27 Years Old
Who Took Home the Most Logo-Emblazoned Oven Mitts.

But if you have stuck around, I finally figured it out. You
know it. The Exit Plan. The seismic career move that will see
me through to retirement and keep me out of a dirty nursing
home.

Every copywriter and art director I know is looking for the
Exit Plan.

Some will open up a frozen yogurt shop. Some will turn to
real estate and sink their money into useless plots of desert
land hoping the government will want to lease it for a solar
panel farm – that's not gonna happen. And some seasoned
veterans will find relief in the chaotic up and down world of
freelancing.

They will discover, as I have, that uncomfortable feeling

walking into a new shop and the staffers glaring, contesting their very presence...

"Is it Bring-Your-Grandparents-To-Work Day?"

Well, those indignities are numbered for this aging creative guy.

You see, I'm transitioning out of copywriting into the new lucrative world of Human Resources. I'm going to create my own job title and offer my services to ad agencies throughout the land as their new Chief Retainment Officer.

You might read this as some harebrained idea from a guy with no head for business. Or simply another comedic vehicle to pad the blog on a slow news day, but I'm completely serious.

Agencies spend a shitload of money trying to attract talent. With the recent Gustavo Martinez debacle at JWT, they're sure to spend even more recruiting women and minorities. They wont have to recruit "Fucking Jews", there are enough of those.

Recruitment is a sizable investment.

But agencies might as well be tossing that money in the toilet. Or the Rich Siegel College Tuition Relief Fund.

Because, let's face it, after 2 years of servitude or the 78th unpaid weekend of Kung Pao Chicken and deck-building, whichever comes first, that "talent" bolts. With it goes all the money the agency has sunk into them: training, relocation fees, and the annexation of adjacent land for the additional parking lot.

Agencies need to find a way to retain what they have worked so hard to recruit.

That's where I come in. Because, perhaps better than most, I know why the disenfranchised are leaving.

As the Chief Retainment Officer, I'm going to fix all that. I'll be the bull in the china shop. Re-aligning briefs. Canceling meetings. And telling clients, "No."

I'll reverse the flow.

Instead of creatives leaving to go elsewhere, they'll be lining up at the door, camped outside, just hoping to get in.

I'll help create the kind of environment that is conducive to great work and pays untold dividends in employee loyalty. My exorbitant salary will be redeemed within months. And agency brass will be kicking themselves wondering why they hadn't contacted me earlier, before their A-list Norwegian rock star creatives packed their bags and herring mason jars and went back to Oslo.

And if all doesn't go according to plan, I can always crank out some banner ads.

Playing with Fire

It has now become a weekly occurrence.

One of the trade magazines, Adweek, AdAge or AgencySpy, will announce the hiring or promotion of one or several executives to high level positions. With it, comes the obligatory, carefully-styled press photo.

If in that photo, there is not one woman, one African American, or one member from the LGBT community (though I don't know how he or she would be possible to identify) the social justice warriors kick it into high gear.

It is as automatic as the folks at WingStop getting my order all wrong.

This is not to say that I don't understand.

I do.

I agree that the business is dominated by young, soft handed, white dudes with an overabundance of lumberjack shirts and stupid over-manicured beard cuts. And I fully concur that the industry would be much improved with a heaping helping of diversity – including some more old people in the Creative Department, I never hear that from the outraged keyboard clackers. Moreover, I also understand that even going near this topic is opening myself up to a torrent of criticism.

Thankfully, I'm getting to a point in my career where I can speak my mind, because frankly I don't give a shit what people want to believe about me.

Truth is, I hear and read a lot of complaining about this scenario, but very little in the way of concrete solutions. Allow me to suggest that the answer may be in gardening.

Gardening?

Yup.

You see an ad agency is like a tree. For it to grow and bear sweet, juicy fruit, it needs pruning.

First, let's get rid of C-Suite Ass Nuggets – People who make rape jokes. Bosses who manage up and never see the people beneath them. Drunks, drug users and anyone, particularly CEO's, who operate with a broken moral compass. Or, more precisely, no moral compass at all. That's a good place to start.

Second, let's identify the redundancies – An account, even a difficult account, does not require a legion of planners. We already have too many cooks in the kitchen. Do we need too many recipes as well? One planner, on one account, should suffice. And if you've been reading RoundSeventeen for any length of time you know that even one, may be one too many.

Third, let's keep identifying redundancies – Sorry to get repetitive, but the planning department is by no means the only culprit. How many times have you walked into a meeting to discuss a banner ad or a down and dirty 15 second spot and been confronted with an army of attendees? What the hell do all these people do? Making Skip Ads is just not that complicated. It's not.

Fourth, let's put the management in Management – How is it that an assignment can change 5 times in the course of two days? Why are the people with MBA's and supposed logistical expertise not able, or willing, to steer a client? And guide them along a well-thought out path towards an agreed-upon goal? I suspect there's more order and efficiency in the governmental offices of Mogadishu in Somalia.

And finally, let's respect our elders – This one is self-explanatory. And if it's not, consider the fact that a tree's growth and sustainability are largely a function of a quality root system.

If we took any or all of these suggestions and pruned wisely, there'd be more room at the top, and everywhere in between for women, African Americans, Asians, Latinos and gay people.

Oh and old guys.

Did I mention old guys?

The Lost Art of Storytelling

Know the difference between a 44-year old copywriter and a 24-year old copywriter?

About 30 seconds.

Allow me to vent, because if I don't get this out of my system my intestines will start a mutiny, half the house will become uninhabitable and my wife, generally of pleasant disposition, will hound me about the placement of my running and hiking shoes in every room but the closet.

As it has been pointed out to me in many private emails and direct messages, I go to great lengths (and possibly take too much pleasure) in pointing out the vocational flaws of my younger colleagues.

I'd love to stop.
Really, I would.
But this one particular grievance happens with such regularity, I dare say it's like clockwork.

I'll be summoned to a creative check in. For you laymen, that's when copywriters and art directors are called upon to genuflect before their superiors – the planners and the account executives – and present the work they have developed, you know, since the last creative check in, 5 hours ago.

It is a fascinating study in agency dynamics, where one can

witness career jockeying, pointless posturing and the full range of modern day office backstabbing techniques. It's also where I get to see the next generation of creatives present their hastily-assembled ideas

When I say "ideas", of course I mean their regurgitated drivel that manages to click off every box and mention every mandatory support point found on the brief.

This is where the inexperience shows. Because the reading of a typical 30 second TV script can often last 7-8 minutes.

You know you're in trouble when you hear the rustling of the paper and the young copywriter takes a breather, a sip of water from his or her $25 hipster water module, and turns to Page Two of the script.

Here's a hint young people. A TV script for a 30 second spot is like a resume, even an over-enhanced resume. It all needs to fit on one page.

Similarly, a 15 second spot should not include more than three "Cut To's." Too many scenes equals too many reasons to Skip Ad or change the channel.

I'm well aware of how this comes off. So let me just say that I, and my many various art director partners, have stepped in the same piles of shit. Our spots were too wordy. Too complicated. And too labored. It's all part of learning the craft.

It's what you do when the client keeps adding messages to the messaging.

The 10 lbs. – now 11 lbs. – must fit in the 5 lbs. bag.

I get it. It's hard to navigate all the various agendas.

It's not easy to say no. And it's even more difficult not to be labeled, "difficult."

Perhaps that's why so many 24 year old staff copywriters become mercenary 44 year old freelance copywriters.

The Circle of Life

One of the things I enjoy about being a freelance copywriter is the variety of assignments. This is especially important to someone like me who is afflicted with ADD, Additional Dollars Desired.

One week, I can be writing about batter-dipped, deep-fried fish sticks and the next I can be doing a white paper on the wisdom of diversified asset management. Last week, I was thrust back into the world of recruitment advertising.

Not exactly the same Help Wanted ads that launched my career at the humble Encino offices of Bernard Hodes Advertising, but not far from it either.

Permit me to take a nostalgic walk into the past to these not-so gloried days.

The mailroom at an ad agency is no place to be. Especially if you have just graduated from college and your parents are hocking you about giving up on this useless dream about being a writer. So when I saw that a recruitment ad agency was looking for a junior writer I sprung into action.

I knew there would be a hundred other applicants for the job. So I told the Creative Director I would do anything for the gig. She gave me a spec assignment and asked how I would go about getting Integrated Systems Engineers in the door at Northrop Aircraft, one of their clients.

I had no idea what Integrated Systems were. Or who
Northrop Aircraft was. Or even what a Help Wanted ad for
an Engineer looked like. This was pre-internet, so I spent
half the weekend at the library. And the other half writing
and coming up with spec ads.

"Tomorrow's challenges, today. At Northrop."

"Join us at our environment for innovation."

"We're engineered for Engineers."

Nothing inspirational. In fact it was all crap.

But the creative director was impressed that I had it on her
desk at 8:30 Monday morning before anyone had even
arrived at the office. I beat out a hundred, maybe two hundred,
other applicants, not because I was better but because I
wanted it more.

Little did I know I'd spend the next two years of my life
cranking out one shitty recruitment ad after another.

Sometimes twenty a day. Dreadful long copy ads about
opportunity, imagination, competitive salaries and
comprehensive dental care.

And now some .....(cough) years later, I am writing
recruitment ads again.

As a friend of mine put it, I have come full circle. I can, with a clear conscience and boatload of debt, go calmly into the light.

2016's Phrase of the Year

I'm not big on re-caps.

The end of 2015 slipped by and I did nothing to rehash the highlights and low lights of the year.

Mostly because I don't think any of you want to relive my life. I made my yearly numbers, I sent two kids off to college, and I had an onion bialy with delicious whitefish salad, blah blah blah.

However, I did coin a phrase in 2016 that is seemingly and unexpectedly gaining some traction. I know this because I have received several emails to the effect. And I've read the comments. And I've seen it repeated with an obligatory Rich Siegel Hat Tip.

Frivolous, Fuckwadian, Digital Knick Knacks™.

Those of you in the ad biz know exactly what I'm referring to. In fact, I'm willing to wager some of you even have a spot in production for this year's Super Bowl. But that spot won't hit the airwaves and thrill 270 million people until you have faithfully completed the 360 degree arc of brand integration.

And that means finishing the social media extension of your big beautiful commercial with some kind of superfluous disposable social media tchotchke™.

What will that be?

* **Tweet To Eat** – Tell us your best Wheat Thin story in 140 characters or less and win a lifetime supply of Wheat Thins, now in Honey Mustard, Chili Cheese and Zesty Salsa (it's zesty.)

* **Free Wheelin'** – Upload your photo and see what your face would look like as a Nissan Hubcap.

* **Meow Mixed** – Post an Instagram of your cat enjoying our delicious, nutritious fish and chicken anal glands and we'll go through your iTunes library and create your very own Meow Mix Mixed Tape.

* **Bud Lights The Way** – Send us your email address, proof of age and access to your GPS and through the magic of Augmented Reality, we will use your mobile phone to direct you to the nearest location where you can buy Bud Light. It's 22nd century technology in the palm of your 21st century hand!

* **The Old Spice Scintillating, Smellolicious Scavenger Hunt** -- Find the tumblr photo of the Old Spice Man on the inter webs, customize the photo so that he is on a goat, retweet the photo and collect 1000 shares, screen grab your customized photo with 1000 shares and at least 10,000 likes, and post it on your Facebook page along with a 3,000 word essay and we'll send you a coupon good for a 15% discount on your next purchase of any Old Spice product.

Those of you not in the business, who often complain that I waste too much digital ink on advertising or advertising-related themes, could care less about these Herculean marketing flim flams which require so much effort and yield so little return – sort of like making crepes.

Fear not advertising laymen, you are in the company of about 8 billion other people who never engage with any of this crap.

And who would frankly be content to live out the rest of their days without ever seeing another *Frivolous, Fuckwadian, Digital Knick Knacks*™.

Lashing Out

Recently, Ad Age published an article titled: 50 Best Places to Work in 2015. I'm happy to say, and not in the slightest pandering way, that I've collected paychecks from five of them: Deutsch, RPA, Sapient Nitro, Team One and M&C Saatchi.

Who says I don't know how to butter that bread?

All due respect to the editors at Ad Age, who refused to give my last book any ink, I think you guys missed the boat.

You see, for my money, and I'm guessing for yours as well, I would have preferred an article about the 50 Worst Places to Work in 2015.

As a freelancer with a dozen years under my belt, plus another twenty as a staffer, I could easily rattle off a list of 50 dysfunctional, mismanaged, political hellholes.

If I drank another cup of coffee I could run the number up to 75. But then I might never work again. My daughters would have to drop out of college. And I'd be reduced to living out my remaining days on store-branded macaroni and cheese and generic vodka.

No. I'm not going to bite the hand that feeds me Wild Caught Alaska King Salmon sold at Whole Foods for only $29.99/lbs. I'm just not.

But I am going to reprint some choice nuggets I found on Glassdoor.com, my new favorite website. And I am going to whip out the magic cloak of anonymity and let you do your own guessing and detective work.

As many of you might know, I have a spur in my spleen about working late or on the weekends and believe strongly in a proper work/life balance. Apparently I'm not alone in this regard. Here's a choice comment from the pages of Glassdoor:

"A lot of people actually sleep here because they don't have time to go home or because it's 5 AM when they are done and it would be too dangerous to drive."

Holy shit!

5AM!

At that hour of the morning I'm in bed, deep in REM sleep and dreaming of Eva Longoria and subliminal train rides through the Lincoln Tunnel.

Here's one of a similar nature, at a different agency.

"Politics get in the way of results. 100 hour work weeks are standard"

100 hours? There are only 168 hours in a week. And I need 43 of them just for blogging, swimming, watching Jeopardy, and fighting with my wife.

This reviewer pulled no punches.

"Management is a hodgepodge of incompetent egos. They try to look like some creative agency but never does any real work. It's all social media stuff and banners. The entire thing is a joke."

Ouch. Not only taking potshots at the agency but also landing a few blows on the fragile chin of digital advertising.

Finally, and perhaps to demonstrate our endless ability to bitch and moan about our chosen profession, there's this from a new employee who takes issue with the agency's unique parking procedures.

"Someone's already scratched my car and it's only been 30 days. This whole valet parking idea is good in theory, terrible in practice."

I could do this all day. But right now there are pressing issues at hand. It seems I have purchased the wrong type of plastic garbage bags and my wife wants to go a few rounds.

Wish me luck.

An Advertising Epiphany

I finally figured it out.

It took me long enough.

Perhaps too long.

Others, smarter than me, got it much earlier in their careers. They worked it. They exploited it. And they regurgitated it enough until the process was as natural as a cow chewing its cud 7 times over.

And these smarter, now wealthier, folks never looked back.

"Spit it out already, Siegel, or I'll turn my attention to AgencySpy, where the design sucks but the comments are still pithy, snarky and to the point."

Ok, here it is.

Clients say they want different. They say they want disruptive. They say they want game-changing. And so we chase our tails, at least I have for far too long, in search of different, disruptive and game-changing.

But that's *not* what they want at all.

They want safe, copy-tested, Twitter-proof ideas that are slickly packaged with the thin veneer of different-ness. The slightest smidgen of unfamiliarity. As Jon Stewart might say, while gesturing like a French chef, just a *soupçon of newness.*

But never enough different, and this is the key, to raise the eyebrow of the public, or worse the CEO, which could trigger attention and the call to the C-Suite headhunter.

"I know she's only been here 6 months, but we need a new CMO."

The problem is, in the era of mass communication, we've been fed such a steady diet of "new and improved" it all feels old and tired. As a result we get food porn, car porn, video game porn, beer commercials that are interchangeable with soda commercials, and limited time Sales Events that are not time limited at all and seem to run 24/7/365.

Doesn't poor Jan from the Toyotathon world ever go on vacation?

Same.
Same.
Same.

Back in 1998, Bill Clinton famously answered a reporters question with...

"That depends on what your definition of is, is."

Having had this little epiphany, I now have a better idea of what *different* is.

Cannes Do

That happened fast.

Seems like it was just yesterday that I was taking my sharp pointy pen to the annual advertising orgy known as the Cannes Festival.

Can an entire year have passed since I sat in my home in Culver City and passed snarky judgment on the fashionistas, hipsters and makers of the world's most treasured advertising, gaudily displayed in the south of France?

How is it possible that the earth made an entire celestial orbit around the sun since we last visited the trinket collectors who have refreshed, changed and pushed the world forward with their monumental achievements in advertising and content creation?

And the panels.

Those precious prescient panels where professional prognosticators predicted the death of television, the birth of robust brand engagement and the re-birth of the banner ad.

If 365 days have come and gone since then, shouldn't we all be knee-deep in conversations with Tostitos, Crest toothpaste and Bounty Paper towels, the quicker picker-upper?

Maybe when you turn 44 years old the clock goes a little

faster because it feels like the ink has barely dried on my 2015 shredding of Cannes. Not to mention 2014, 2013 and the scathing thought piece of 2012, wherein I tackled:

Stingy brim fedoras

Capri pants

Rosé wine

Company yachts

Elitism

Over-promoted, under-skilled agency brass

The 5,000 mile international boundary for permissible infidelity

The Gutter Bar

V-neck T-shirts

The tone-deaf Facebook postings of rampant agency debauchery while homebound "team members" forfeit their nights and weekends to assemble PDF's of decks that will digitally transverse the ocean only to remain gleefully unzipped.

Even though I relish the opportunity to take thinly-veiled potshots at the industry and the greedy gluttons who have so diligently earned the disdain of their colleagues, it just seems so done.

Doing another blog piece on the excesses of the festival feels tired. And repetitive. And meaningless. And wasteful. And self-important.

Wait a minute.

Could this lazy, repackaged regurgitation of past work be the perfect metaphor for Cannes and the current state of advertising?

When Hate is Good

How do I know if an idea is good?

I know it, when someone hates it.

Last week I was driving to the Sport Chalet in Marina del Rey. On the way home, on picturesque Alla Drive, there is a focus group facility. The same facility I used to attend with great regularity, when I was a staffer. The same facility, where thanks to my big, unfiltered mouth, I cavalierly blew $25,000 worth of BBDO research money.

We were conducting two groups and testing some concepts we were going to pitch in a heavily contested battle for LA Cellular, a large and now-defunct telecom.

The first group was a disaster.

Of Hindenburgian proportion.

Before the second group commenced, I went to get some much needed coffee. As I was refilling my cup, I turned to the facility moderator and blurted:

"Send in the next bunch of losers."

Unaware, perhaps, that the next bunch of losers were sitting in the adjacent room. The room with the open door. The room that was filled with people who could hear the cap being torn off the little creamer and poured into my awaiting cup. Yeah, those losers.

The night didn't end well.
Our ideas for the pitch didn't go well.
And my short stint at BBDO grew even shorter.

You might assume from this little anecdote that I have no love for Focus Groups. And I don't. But in hindsight I know the problem isn't about research. It's about how clients interpret research.

Let's say Concept A is shown to a group of folks who have nothing better to do on a Tuesday night than to sit with a bunch of demographically similar people and judge prospective TV commercials which they will dutifully fast forward through on their DVRs. And let's say 90% of the group likes Concept A. And 10% of the group doesn't like it.

Let's also say that these same people, who seem very content with crappy lasagna and free M&M's are shown Concept B.

The response here is more visceral. 60% of the group hates it and would, if they could, throat punch the creators of Concept B until they begged for mercy. The other 40% of the group love the idea and might even consider tweeting about it.

Well, marketing executives are like Doomsday Preppers. They will do anything to insure their survival.

So when it comes time to decide, they're going with their mortgages, their private school tuitions and their $499 a month lease payments on their new Lexus GS; they're going with Concept A.

After all, 90% of the people polled sort of liked it. You can't argue with that. If my phone were 90% charged or my daughter got a 90% on a history test or my brake pads still had 90%, I'd be thrilled.

But in the arena of mass communication, of breaking through the clutter, of intentionally polarizing people in order to get a reaction or influence behavior, a tepid 90% is 100% wrong.

If it were up to me, and for a thousand good reasons it never is, I would go with Concept B.

Or, to misquote John Lennon, "Hate is all we need."

An Exciting Career in Advertising

There are times when I feel obliged to give something back to advertising, an industry that has given me so little.

Last week was one of those times.

I don't remember (which is not all surprising these days) who had asked me to sit on a panel at Santa Monica High School's Career Day, but for some unknown reason they did. Conveniently ignoring the fact that technically, as a freelancer, I am unemployed. And have been for more than a dozen years.

Nevertheless, if someone was going to give me my own souvenir name badge, a snazzy lanyard and my own Vikings-emblazoned sippy cup, who was I to turn down such swag?

My initial inclination was to ironically show up for Career Day sporting a T-shirt, cargo shorts and flip flops. To show these kids that you could make a decent living in the business world in attire that was very un-businesslike. My wife dissuaded me of this notion. And I slapped on some monkey clothes.

However, upon my arrival I was greeted by my buddy, Paul, who is an English teacher at Samohi. He was wearing a t-shirt, cargo shorts and flip flops.

As I pushed my way through the crowded hallways, before

the 3rd period panel, I was naturally reminded of my own days in high school – a messy collage of good times, bad times, laughter, sadness, adolescent confusion, drug experimentation, and enough unused testosterone to fuel two penises.

In other words, typical.

I mention this because as I looked over the 30-40 kids in the room, I spotted the same neuroses.

Sadly, my fellow panelists did not. Their understanding of what a Career Day at a high school is, differed greatly than mine.

The woman seated next to me, a branding, PR consultant officer with multiple degrees in finance and marketing, took the time to prepare a robust Powerpoint presentation.

Fortunately, the hour time limit prevented her from abusing us all with that little gem. But she was able to monopolize the discussion and when it came time to inspire these kids, she never failed to fail.

"Has anybody here ever heard of Metric Analytics? Well, I've done a little research on your behalf and you'll be happy to know that in the next 10 years there will be 1.5 million excellent jobs in the field of Metric Analytics."

Are you kidding me?

When I was able to wedge in a word I made sure to give them the flip side to her enticing tales of Big Data, Bell Curves and Pie Charts.

I told them how much fun it was to travel in Business Class, stay in fancy hotels, and raid the mini-bar starting with the $12 Toblerone Chocolates and working your way through the Jack Daniels airplane bottles all the way to the $22 jar of Deluxe Mixed Nuts.

I talked about having celebrities act out your jokes on film, playing golf on the company dime, flying in private jets and sitting in the booth next to Johnny Carson at Chaya Playa.

They had never heard of Johnny Carson.

The point is, these were 16 year old kids. They needed to be shown some razzle dazzle. I put myself in their shoes, the same shoes I was walking in just 28 years ago. I wanted to keep it light on industry specifics and heavy on boondoggles, graft and free alcohol.

Ms. Bataan Death Powerpoint wanted to babble on about analytics, segmentation and PR Crisis Management. Oh, for Christ's sake.

I could tell the students were bored. But the best indication came at 11:34 when the bell rang. There was no applause, no thanks, no students lingering on to ask questions and maybe dig in a little further into the exciting world of emerging social media demographics. They simply swiveled around in their plastic desk/chair and bolted for their next class.

I had to get home to work on some freelance assignments. So, on the way back to my car and still fuming over this colossal waste of my time, I walked by the career day greeting area that had been set up for the incoming panelists. There, and without the least bit of guilt, I helped myself to an additional blue Samohi Career Day sippy cup.

Which means some well-intentioned fireman or astronaut went home with none.

Sorry.

Brand Engorgement

Pretty soon we'll be celebrating the 20 year anniversary of the internet.

Which means you (well, not my daughters because they're under 20 and they don't read "*Daddy's boring blog*" or "*Daddy's deadly books*") and I have been around for every kb of it.

Personally, I have spent a great deal of time on the internet, probably a lot more than I should have. But as I write for a living, I'm sort of tied to my keyboard. And the keyboard is irresistibly linked to the web.

But here's the thing, in all those twenty years, I have spent virtually none of it engaged with any brands. None.

OK, there was one time that VW put out this racing game that could be played on the iPhone or the iPad and I did that for about 5 minutes. But the game was such a poor version of Gran Turismo I dumped it immediately.

I certainly didn't come away from the experience with any greater sense of Fahrvergnügen. Or any greater appreciation of VW. If anything, I was disappointed. And vowed to never get sucked into any more of this digital nonsense.

I know others have written passionately on this topic. And

because they are better writers, they are able to provide academic proof and literary references that are far above my pay grade.

I speak anecdotally. Mostly to accommodate my facile thinking.

And as the father of two teenage girls (who are decidedly in the sweet spot for many of these digitally-obsessed companies) I can attest that they too are equally unimpressed by these brand engagement efforts.

I know because I asked them point blank. They cocked their heads and looked at me the same bewildered way my dog looks at me when I pour a bowl of cereal out of a box.

"Why would we spend time with any of that? That's advertising. Advertising sucks."

Completely oblivious to my line of work or the fact that advertising – that is the making of advertising – has paid for every gadget, every morsel of food, every remote control, every shoe and every stick of furniture in the house.

"So what, it still sucks."

If this sentiment ended here, so would this little essay. But my daughter's friends say the same exact thing. And so do their friends. There are 1.5 billion videos on YouTube they'll counter, who has time for advertising gimmicks?

Which has got me wondering.

I know there are hundreds, if not thousands, of people in ad agencies and on the client side, spending millions of dollars and countless man hours building elaborate digital brand engagement schemes. Everyday we're out there Tweeting and Vining and Instagramming and UXing and HTMLing.

Or as my pal George says, "we're making toys."

The question is, who's playing with them?

I Am Not Veal

My contempt for the open office plan is as endless as the new Endless Table recently installed at the Barbarian Group in NYC.

If you hadn't read about it, the Endless Table or SuperDesk™ is a ¼ mile long loop of concrete tabletop. It was designed by the same world class architect who designed the offices of TBWA Chiat/Day, a place I used to call home for so many years.

I loved working at the Big Yellow House in Playa Vista, just 2.7 miles from my home. Mainly because we had the semblance of a real office, an in-house restaurant, a basketball court and state of the art editing and production facilities, all in the same building.

What we didn't have was an 1,100 foot long concrete, rebar-reinforced monstrosity ribboning through the office posing as some advancement in advertising office ergonomics.

I don't fault the architect.

In fact, thanks to some mutual friends in the industrial design arena, he and I are only separated by two degrees. So, if this should ever get back to him, he should know I am a big admirer of his work.

He was only doing what we all try to do – deliver on

the brief.

I have a bigger problem with the agency brass who have deluded themselves into thinking that creativity can thrive in a tiny (4 ft.) workspace more suited to an abattoir-bound baby cow.

You might hear a lot of claptrap about "greater collaboration" and the "spontaneous free-flowing spark of imagination", but I'm here to tell you it's all bullshit. Mouthed by millennial sycophants who have been spoon-fed a steady diet of architectural malarkey and trained to speak in jargon-filled vagaries.

This isn't just me blowing off some old man smoke.

If you've got a few minutes and your co-worker next to you isn't blasting some horrendous European electronica crap through his or her Dr. Dre Beatphones, or whatever the hell they call them, you should scour through the archives of the New Yorker. There's a telling article that details, at length, the decline of productivity and morale in today's modern new gulags.

Or watch how quickly the agency secluded war rooms get booked up first thing in the morning. Squatted on by veterans who know that thinking and creating require peace and quiet.

Or, here's an even better idea.

If you're curious and would like to know why the big wigs at the Barbarian Group would drop $300,000 on an Endless Table instead of, oh I don't know, using that money to create a more private, more humane, more productive work environment, why don't you ask them?

They should be stepping out of their closed-door offices any minute now.

Confessions of a Mercenary

I spent the majority of my career in advertising as a staff guy.

Or as I often say, a chump.

When I was on the company payroll, I never cared for those carefree freelancers who would arrive at the last minute after all the legwork had been done and 16 rounds of work had been killed.

And it didn't help that they'd stroll into the office with their come-in-at-11 attitude. Or their I'm-shoving-out-at-4-and-there's-nothing-you-can-do-about-it end of day demeanor.

Who were these "happy" creatives and what business did they have with our business? I often thought.

You can chalk it up to being young, insecure and overly ambitious, but we staffers also regarded the hiring of freelancers as a not-so-subtle signal from upper management. That they had lost confidence in our ability to come up with a creative solution and needed the high-priced professional gunslingers to come in and clean up our mess.

Or so, we thought.

But now I'm 44 and have been playing for the other team for more than 10 years. I have another perspective on the matter. In fact, and I say this with no self-serving agenda whatsoever, I believe freelancers will be the ones who save our industry.

Here's why.

Freelancers are cheaper than staffers. They can telecommute. They require no real estate footprint. They demand no benefits. Think how much money is wasted on the false camaraderie of employee picnics, birthday cakes, and Secret Santas. This country would be back in the black if businesses, large and small, didn't have to reach into their pocket and shell out billions of dollars for supermarket cupcakes and bi-annual employee dental cleanings.

They're also cheaper because you only pay them when there is work to be done. These days that work can be sporadic.

Clients are moving away from the AOR model and doing more project work. And that project work is often doled out as a "jump ball." Pitting one holding company agency against a sister agency.

It goes without saying if you find yourself in a jump ball situation, you want to deploy the "tallest, most athletic" creative team money can buy. Tall and athletic being a metaphor for bald and stocky, of course.

Also, freelancers are easier. There's no drama. No trauma. And no "Why do I always get the shitty assignments? Why don't you give this pharma project to Bill and Kathy, they're the ones that dropped the meat in the dirt on the last new business pitch?"

Freelancers are happy to work on any project. From a mammoth Super Bowl spot to the continued evolution of the Crestor Guy.

"The client wants Crestor Guy to be more three dimensional. With a more urgent call to action. Maybe even have him do some live tweeting."

"Pffft, no problem," said the eager freelancer.

And finally there's this. Freelancers are more efficient.

You hand the brief to a freelance team, hold a gun up to their head and say you need to see something in a day and 24 hours later that freelance team will have a packet or a PDF of fresh new ideas. That's just the way it works.

Wham, bam, thank you Omnicom.

Then, on Friday afternoon, when the account team comes back from the presentation and announces all the work has died, the freelancers will be right there to pick up the slack. Ready to fire up the meter, work the weekend and charge double overtime. There's no pouting. Or grousing. Or venting via the comment section on AgencySpy.

Because to a freelancer there's only one phrase sweeter than *"the strategy has changed."*

"The check has cleared."

Vocational Viagra

Let's talk about job title inflation.

It's not the first time I've written about it and it probably won't be the last, as it is growing faster than Alec Baldwin's waistline.

Not long ago, I promoted myself to Chairman of the Rich Siegel Worldwide organization. First, because we can never have too many corporate chairmen in this world. Secondly, to point out the ridiculous nature of workplace nomenclature. And thirdly, as if we needed a thirdly, a promotion, even a meaningless one, can go a long way to sooth the insatiable need for validation.

The fact of the matter is I'm not a chairman, I'm a copywriter.

I don't need any further Orwellian newspeak attached to that title in order to impress anybody. And frankly when I come across people who roll out the Senior Vice President or Chief Officer or Executive Group Global Blah Blah Blah, I'm not impressed.

If anything I'm unimpressed – there should be a better word for that – I'm depressed.

In my fantasy utopian world where everything I say is right and everyone who thinks otherwise is not, I would roll back all this title nonsense.

Let's say a kid graduates from one of the outrageously expensive advertising schools littered throughout the land.

And let's say he or she wants to pursue a career in copywriting.

And let's say he or she is genuinely talented but still has a long way to go.

And let's take this theoretical situation even further and say he or she has the goods to get immediately hired.

The first job out of the box should be Apprentice Copywriter. Because let's face it, he or she knows nothing about how ads are done in the real world.

With a few banner ads and FSI's under his or her belt, the first promotion should be to Junior Assistant Copywriter.

In a year's time, maybe two, and the writing of some solid emails blasts, internal videos and sizzle pieces, the word Junior can magically disappear.

Maybe the stars aligned and our talented aspiring writer managed to knock out a case study or even a radio spot or a print ad, then our Assistant Copywriter can proudly call home and start adjusting the linkedin page to include Associate Copywriter.

Finally, after earning some industry cred and earning the respect (and jealousy) of others, then, and only then, would he or she be given the title of Copywriter.

It's title deflation.

Not only is it more logical, it prevents those uncomfortable new business meetings when the CEO of a multi-billion dollar corporation is seated next to a 26-year old tattooed, pierced, keffiyeh-wearing clod who goes by the title, Senior EVP Group Content Curation Prophet.

Oh Advertising, You Amuse Me

Last week was Advertising Week in New York City. And for the 29th year in a row, I was not in attendance.

As you might expect as a bona fide Kool-Aid hater, I'm not a big fan of conferences, confabs, symposiums, or any type of large gathering that might require me to pee in a stainless steel trough. I have no interest in any activity that necessitates a printed schedule and wall-to-wall panels and forums.

*6:45 — **10 Reasons Why You're Not Flying Business Class***

*7:50 — **Sweat Shop Architecture, How to Maximize Profits by Minimizing Employee Workspace***

*8:35 — **Pizza, The Best and Least Expensive Way To Feed Overtime Workers***

Now, I've got to tread lightly here.

Jerry Seinfeld recently gave a scathing speech at an advertising award show and was roundly criticized for his demeaning and snarky tone. He and I share many of the same views on the industry, though his perspective is quite different than mine.

He's a gazillionaire comedian who can afford to bite the

hand that feeds him. Hell, if he wanted he could buy Omnicom and Publicis and stage Celebrity CEO Death Matches.

I also like to nibble on the hand that feeds me, but I'm a considerably less-wealthy freelance copywriter and can't afford to exacerbate the situation – as Jerry did – by also shitting on the victim's bloodied handless stump.

Truth is, advertising has been, and continues to be, very, very good to me. I've been able to make a decent living simply by being a wise ass. It's like I never left high school.

My problem with Advertising Week and all these expensive extravaganzas, and that includes SXSW, Cannes, etc., is the artifice of it all. It's the willful pretending that what we do, is not what we do.

We're not starting conversations.

No one in their right mind wants to have a conversation with Febreeze.

We're not giving brands a distinctive voice.

The voice of Burger King sounds remarkably like the voice of McDonalds. *"Please come in and eat our processed meat-thingies."*

And we're not making the world a better place.

15 minutes could save you 15% or more on car insurance.

For every ground shaking noteworthy campaign, like the rebirth of Apple or the meteoric rise of Old Spice, there are 10,000 efforts, maybe 100,000, that made no one smile, cry, laugh, or even think. They had zero powers of persuasion. In fact, because they were an insult on intelligence and so poorly crafted, it is more likely these campaigns dissuaded consumers.

You'll never see a panel on that.

The reality is, and 99% of my colleagues who work in the trenches and also never go to these "festivals" will agree, our business is about moving the merchandise.

So when the client says we need to find a better way to say,

"There's never been a better time to visit your _____ dealer."

We schedule meetings, do focus groups, write briefs, explore creative alternatives, and then we find a better way to say,

"There's never been a better time to visit your _____ dealer."

Or, we just go with what the client wanted.

That's the business we're in.

The Tale of the Thin Packet

War story time.

Years ago I was hired to do a freelance gig. It was a one week affair. A run and gun, drink some coffee, bring an extra set of clothes, bitch of a pitch.

I'm not very fond of these affairs and never believed the best creative is produced under these conditions. But, as my niece – a guidance counselor – once pointed out in a book of job definitions for graduating high schoolers, a Copywriter must be able to sparkle on demand.

On this particular job I was teamed up with another copy-writer. That doesn't happen too often but he was a colleague and someone I had known for many years. He's also one of the few people who can hold his own in a battle of wits, despite being raised in Wisconsin.

We were briefed at 9:30 AM and by 9:45 AM had fallen into a comfortable rhythm.

We were riffing.

Writing.

And sparkling on demand.

We maintained this scorching pace throughout the day.

Interrupted by several bitch sessions about being married, fathering children, scummy Hollywood agents, other hacky copywriters, and again about being married.

At 6 o'clock we got a phone call from the creative director who had briefed us just 9 hours earlier. He was offsite but wanted to see the work. And told us to email everything we had by the end of the day.

So we stopped looking at Turkish Bestiality Porn and knocked out a couple of more scripts.

At 8 PM, we hit the Send button, a hastily-written note and 16 fully written scripts. That was some serious sparkling.

The very next morning we approached the swaggering creative director and solicited some feedback.

"The packet was a little thin."

That was his response. Verbatim.

16 scripts. One day.

And the packet was a little thin!

I thought we were in the business of solving a client's business challenge with strategic, disruptive communications, I didn't get the memo we were now in business of pumping out marketing manure by the pound.

As if that doesn't defy logic, consider our reactions.

I, born and bred in New York, wanted to clock this ass-nugget and share with him some of the wisdom I've learned in my 44 years on this earth. But I bit my lip and smiled.

My Wisconsin compatriot was even more steamed.

"The packet was thin," he muttered under his breath.

Sensing his anger, I wedged my body between my midwestern colleague and the shit-for-brains Creative Director. You probably don't know many people from Wisconsin, but I'm here to tell you, they're preternaturally nice and usually not prone to violence.

Usually.

But pacifism prevailed.

In the end, none of the 87 scripts we wrote that week made it into the 534-page deck presented to the client. And the agency we were working for, didn't win the pitch. In fact they had their pockets picked and lost the account.

Two hardworking, hard sparkling copywriters enjoyed a hardy hot bowl of schadenfreude.

The Cannes-gover

If you happen to be employed in advertising you know today is the Worst. Day. Ever.

Why?

Because today the adverati return from Cannes. Most will come home empty-handed, but full of glory-hungry piss and vinegar. They watched as the Brazilians and Europeans carted off a suitcase packed with lions and vowed to return next year with work that would knock your $200 Fedora off.

And so today, the creatives who didn't go to France to lounge on a yacht, sip rosé wine and pontificate about the holistic integration of Instagram, Twitter, and wearable anklet computers, the ones who banged out the sales events, the statement stuffers and the e-mail blasts that keep the lights on, will get an earful.

You know what I'm talking about: The Pep Talk.

Years ago we would have been herded into the conference room. But now, since we all sit at the community table or the SuperDesk™, the flagellation…er, motivational speeches can be administered out in the open.

"We have to be smarter."

"We have to work harder."

"We have to generate ideas faster."

"We have to take our client's $37,000 budget and make it seem like $37 million. We can do this. You can do this. Make it happen people. I'm going to lunch."

Stop me if you've heard this before. Chances are you have. And you'll hear it again next year. Because the powers that be in advertising, the ones who graced you with a 2 inch high Eiffel Tower souvenir from their annual French boondoggle, are averse to change.

The only change they're interested in is an upgraded suite at the InterContinental Carlton in 2017.

But I'm an outsider now. And have no vested interest in vesting. Or ladder climbing. And, perhaps blindly, no fear of retribution.

So here's my humble but deadly-accurate prescription, for agencies that want to win awards at Cannes.

1.) **Pink Slip The Planners** – You show me a creative team that can't figure out a distinctive market insight and I'll show you a team that doesn't deserve a Cannes Lion. Or a job for that matter.

2.) **Put Creatives in Charge** – The final say on what goes out the door and sold to the client goes to a Creative Director. Not a CEO, a CMO, or a CFO. Or worse, a committee of all the aforementioned.

3.) **Never say the words Social and Media in the same sentence** – Banners, tweets, mobile apps, Facebook updates, page takeovers, kickstarters, Tumblrs and Foursquare friend finders have never sold a single widget, doohickey or whatchamacallit. They never will. Stop. Just stop.

4.) **Make with the Funny** – With the exception of Barton Graf and the agency doing the Geico ads, there are few folks doing work that's genuinely funny. Not wink worthy. Or smile inducing. People want ads that makes them laugh.

4a.) **Hire a crusty Old Time Writer** – In the 13 years I've been freelancing I haven't been to one agency that couldn't benefit from an old timey writing guy. Or gal. Who knows how to put one word in front of another and bring back the art of persuasion.

5.) **Finally, Burn the Community Table** – Writers and art directors need offices. Real offices with doors and windows and a little mini-fridge where they can keep their beer. Give them the offices formerly occupied by the planners.

Pick One

Have you ever thought about ditching your life as an ad agency staffer and exploring the wonderful, carefree existence of a freelancer?

A life full of rainbows, unicorns and fat, tax-free paychecks.

Or maybe the shoe is on the other foot.

Have you ever yearned to crawl back into the agency world and cozy up to a full time gig with free bagels, paid vacations and an endless supply of three ring binders?

It's quite the dilemma. And it probably gets discussed more in the hallways of an ad agency than that other proverbial discussion about the "asshat client with all the vision of a ground mole."

I know this to be true because I've batted for both teams. In fact, soon I'll be celebrating 13 mostly-successful years as a freelancer. Before that, were more years than I care to think of as a full time ad guy sucking on the corporate teat.

A couple of months ago I received an email from a friend in NY, who shall remain nameless, but whose story is quite universal.

He was going through a rough patch in his career, meaning he had to work on a day that ended in a "Y", and was envious of my position as a hired gun.

What he didn't know was, that with no apparent reason, my phone had suddenly stopped ringing.

One day off turned into one week off. One week off turned into a fortnight. And a fortnight with no visible stream of revenue turned into mild panic disorder. With nightmares of my family eating out of a dumpster and me in a dirty nursing home with Jamaican orderlies pilfering my loose change and my Vicodin.

The point is, there's enough *tsuris* for everyone. Staffers have to sit in the middle seat on a last minute flight to Des Moines.

Freelancers have to sit in a janitor's closet, jerry-rigged to be an office.

Staffers have to listen to junior clients tell them why the work is off strategy.

Freelancers have to watch Montel Williams tell tattooed amateur rappers they are the father.

Staffers have to smile through pep talks, status meetings and employee reviews that always end in, "there's no money for raises or bonuses."

Freelancers have to endure spouses and children yammering,

"when are you going to get a real job?"

In short, the grass isn't always greener on the other side.

It's brown, it's full of weeds and it's often littered with the unwanted business of the neighbor's dog. So it boils down to picking the lesser of two evils.

For me, I'd prefer the poison of a freelancer.

Back to the dry spell.

Eventually, as it always does, the phone did ring, multiple times. And like a schmuck I ended up taking the gig with the lowest day rate.

The Ridiculous Practice of Over-Employment

The presidential campaign is picking up steam. With the wars in the Middle East winding down, gas prices falling, and morality issues being cleared from the table (rightfully so) it looks like it's all going to come down to the issue of jobs.

Democrats and Republicans agree, there aren't enough of them.

I disagree.

I think there are too many.

We don't need to add more people to the payroll.
We need to remove more work from the workplace.

Admittedly, I can't speak with any authority about other industries, but in the ad agency world, I know from which I speak.

I have spent the better part of the last 30 years bopping around from ad agency to ad agency. I get to see all their stark differences. Some have in-house coffee from Starbucks, others from Peets, and still others from Dunkin Donuts.

And I get to see their similarities.

This list is considerably longer.

Despite all the company hoo-ha about "our dynamic and proprietary storytelling process", "our ability to surround the consumer with unique and disruptive communication" or "our unmatched creativity and global resources", all ad agencies are the same. The holding companies have seen to that.

This parity allows me to point my fat, clubby finger not at any one individual agency but at the industry as a whole. And lately, it's less about the work and more about the work of the work.

Within the last 6 months, I've seen decks about decks, videos about videos, and sat in meetings about other meetings. I don't know how it works, but there must be profit in all this process.

It now takes a hundred people to do the work of ten.

I'm not a process/bureaucracy/let's-build-consensus-kind of guy. I'm not really interested in the opinions of junior account people, junior clients or junior planners. If they had valuable input they wouldn't be juniors, would they?

That's why I enjoy having a blog. And turning those blog posts into books.

I write it.
I publish it.
You read it.

Sometimes I'll even double check it for typos, but that's it.

Of course in the 8 years I've been blogging, I haven't made a dime.

Not one red cent.

Maybe I need to hire an assistant?

Jacob's Ladder

Don't know about you, but I make it a point to stay on top of industry news.

It's good to know which companies are losing accounts. And which companies are winning accounts – which they will no doubt lose once the "branding" campaign fails to generate more than 138 Facebook likes or 79 YouTube views and franchisees/dealers/VC investors demand the agency start moving the needle.

But as I tell other freelancers, or creatives who are forced to freelance because they Got Quit, turmoil is your best friend.

It's also good to stay abreast on who is getting promoted.

Last week, I noticed several folks took on new and semi-important titles. I'm sure these promotions were followed by celebratory mylar balloons, nominal social media congratulations from jealous colleagues and a lot of mouth diarrhea from the Executive Suite:

"Congratulations, you now have the title and responsibilities of a Group Creative Director. But uh...we don't have any more money for you. We've all got to tighten the belt. I'll tell you more about your new job when I come back from Cannes."

Who wouldn't want to get promoted, right?

Well, it's taken me 44 years, but I'm here to tell you it's all Fool's Gold.

Particularly in the creative department of an agency, where the goal is to be the one who decides what gets shown (and hopefully sold) to the client and what gets left in a deck that will never be seen by anyone but the janitorial staff.

Guess what Mr. or Ms. Young Group Creative Director, you're not the one making those important decisions. And neither is the guy or gal above you. Or even above them.

In fact, unless you have your name on the door and your mugshot is the first one people see on the agency website, you have no more voice in the matter than the Assistant Associate Content Strategist, who only last year was organizing the bake sale at University of Wisconsin chapter of Kappa Kappa Gamma.

In today's world of advertising, and this happens in every agency from Portland, Maine to Portland, Oregon, the Chief Creative Officer is a not an officer at all.

He or she is a Committee.
A Council.
A Partnership.
A Board.
A Panel.
A Bureau.
A Conclave.
A Tribunal.
A Junta.

And I've only reached the third paragraph of the online thesaurus.

Years ago, you would hear many agency people derisively call Focus Groups, Fuck-Us Groups.

In our collective race to the bottom, we have successfully pre-empted those soul-sucking gatherings of know-it-all housewives and tuna fish sandwich hoarding dads, and internalized our own everyone-gets-a-voice, politburo-like processes.

Yeah, Go Team!

On the death of creativity, I have seen the enemy.

And it is us.

Talent Crises? What Crisis?

I'm seeing a lot of chatter lately on the interwebs from
Recruitment people…er, I'm sorry, Talent Acquisition
Officers, regarding the best way for ad agencies to attract
and retain top creative talent.

Apparently there's a crisis in adland and many writers and
art directors are foregoing a career on the agency side and
opting instead for the promising world of start up techs. Or
the cash rich giants of Silicon Valley and Silicon Beach:
Facebook, Google and Amazon.

The crisis, I believe, is self-generated.

It doesn't take a rocket scientist or a Leadership Committee
or even a prankish stunt at the recent Cannes Festival to put
this puppy to rest.

All it takes is some common sense.
Mmmmm, where are we going to find that?

As an under-employed, underachieving freelance copywriter, I
feel I have the specious credentials to speak on the matter.
After all, I did spend the first two inglorious years in the
business writing recruitment ads.

And the rest of my "career" hop-scotching from agency to
agency in search of the ideal environment. Or a better
commute. Or just a better assortment of soft drinks in the
vending machine.

If I were in the business of nabbing the best and the brightest for an agency, here's what I would offer:

An office. You want to be in the business of coming up with ideas for America's Fortune 500 companies? We're going to give you the space to do it. With a window, a door and a desk large enough to accommodate a surreptitious afternoon nap. No AmazingDesks™, no shoulder-to-shoulder picnic tables, no need for Bose Noise Canceling headphones to put over your Beats Noise Canceling headphones. You're welcome.

Nights. They belong to you. We believe that after you've put in a hard day of ideating or content creation or emojifying, your brain needs to shut down. The doors at the agency close at 7. So you get home by 8. To see your kids. Your husband. Your wife. And the rest of your life. Clients need to be told that last minute changes do not get last minute solutions. Thinking requires time. Good night.

Weekends. See above. Saturdays and Sundays also belong to you. However, certain situations may create the need for more of your time. Clients don't expect us to give our time away for free and we don't expect you too either. If we bring you in on the weekend, we will pay you extra for the weekend. Seems fair, right?

A Bitch of a Pitch. Pitching new business can be exciting, nerve-wracking, exhausting, career-changing and exhausting. It should also be rewarding. If we pitch new business and we win new business, the holding company officers in New York will take home a little taste. We think you should too.

It's that simple. Here's your envelope.

The Work. Finally, because we offer people an unprecedented environment for creativity, an environment you won't find anywhere else in the agency world, we expect, no, we demand the kind of work that you won't find anywhere else in the agency world. We believe great work generates more great work. You deliver on your end, we'll deliver on ours.

Produce great work and you get to keep your office, your nights, your weekends and your bonuses.

Don't produce great work and you'll find yourself at another agency, sitting at the long table at 4 AM, eating cold Chicken Curry and wondering how to tell the art director next to you that she has to find a new deodorant.

See how that works?

Let's Review the Review

If you reside in Adland you are well aware of the creative and media review initiated by AT&T, the nation's largest... er, I don't even know what to call them anymore.

Their account is worth $438 billion dollars, equivalent to the GDP of China, Russia and Finland, combined.

Normally I'd be itching to get in on that good freelance action. I'm sure agencies are paying top dollar for mercenary creatives like myself to dig in with both hands and crack the code that will lead to victory.

But that turns out to be my naiveté speaking.

Last week I was reading about the review as reported on AgencySpy, which is quickly becoming the only legitimate news source for the industry. Equally enlightening are the AgencySpy comments left by trollers, recently fired employees, and surprisingly enough, people in the know.

Apparently, there is no code to be cracked.

The contest, between two mighty holding companies, will not be decided based upon 20th century criteria like creativity, design or strategic thinking. That's so passe.

No, like the way anything gets done in America, it will depend on cronyism, favor taking, margin trimming, and huge sums of money being passed under the table. Or in the Champagne Room at the Rack Shack.

You see, it's no longer about storyboards, scripts or anthems that carve out a unique point of view. That's all been commoditized. So much so that unlike days of yore when you could tell a Chiat/Day or Wieden & Kennedy spot from a JWT or McCann Erikson spot, now it all looks and feels the same.

And that's fine, let the bean counters have their day.

It's a sweet, savory reversal of fortune.

Because in the long feverish days and nights leading up to the pitch, I hope it's the creatives who get to go home at 5.

And I hope it's the finance folks and the holding company execs who are eating Mushu Pork at 1 AM or assembling the Powerpoint decks on a hot Saturday afternoon without *any fuckin' air conditioning!!!*

Sitting in Judgment

It's award season in advertising again.

I think we all know that from the flood of tweets and pictures from Cannes appearing on our Facebook feeds.

"Look, there's that Mucketty Muck Creative Director who didn't approve my Super Bowl spot. Doesn't he look like he's having a good time in his plaid shorts and his $120 Calvin Klein Crew Neck T-Shirt. I hope he drinks too much rosé wine, eats some bad snails and blows chunks all over that CFO who tried to idiot-splain why the agency didn't have any money this year - or the past 5 years -- for bonuses, raises or new computers to replace the 2007 MacBooks. Oh and look, they're on a yacht."

Wait, where was I before I got diverted onto my tired Bernie Sanders like rant about the financial inequality plaguing the ad industry?

Oh yes, awards.

Well, before they can hand out the trinkets, trophies and metallic validation of our oh-so-disposable Skip Ads and Viral Stunts, there's an award-judging season.

That's when cream of the crop creatives, from all over the land, are flown to exotic locations to sit in imperial favor and cast their discerning eyes on who and what shall be admitted to their inner circle.

Here too, we are often treated to a photographic collage of their international adventures via social media.

They're in Aruba.
In Fiji.
In Greece.
In Havana.

Any destination that manages to skirt the agency's restrictive rule on flying Business Class and earns these prestigious judges their precious pre-flight warmed chocolate chip cookie.

I use the term cream of the crop creatives because it is a status I have successfully avoided.

Oh, I came close in my day, but was always denied entry. In many ways it's like a high school cafeteria. I never sat with the football players and the cheerleaders, but occasionally managed to pull up a stool next to the lacrosse team equipment manager or the flag twirlers.

That is not to say that I have never been asked to judge a show.

A dozen years ago, I was invited to partake in the decision making for the Pele Awards. Never heard of them? Neither had I. Turns out they are a second tier local awards show for our ad colleagues living in Hawaii.

It rained the three days we were there.

Apparently the Motel 6 was booked to capacity and my wife and I were put up at the Royal Illikai in the heart of Waikiki. There was nothing remotely royal about the place. And as we joked later, while fighting off food poisoning from some room service spicy tuna poke, they managed to put the ILL in ILLIKAI.

As recently as 8 months ago, I was asked to judge another show. I can't even remember who it was for. I do remember that the work sucked and, even better, the judging was all accomplished online.

Fueling my wife's oft-heard complaint, "We never leave Culver City."

It Doesn't Keep Going and Going and Going

Last night, while watching the NBA Finals, Jeff Van Gundy had this to say about small forward 35 year old Richard Jefferson, a guy who usually comes off the bench...

"He's amazing. Got this limitless, deep well of energy, I swear he's like the Energizer Bunny."

A truly remarkable statement considering the Energizer Bunny stopped being like the Energizer Bunny years ago.

If you'll recall the Bunny made its debut by busting through staid, formulaic commercials. You, the viewer, would get sucked into believing you were watching some terrible spot about a nasal spray, a body soap or a performance sedan, and then via the Fourth Wall, the Bunny would burst through and take the steaming piss out of the whole thing.

The underlying message: the batteries were so strong and so long lasting (qualities one wants in a battery) that the Bunny could not be stopped and would just Keep Going. And going. And going.

In the parlance of the day, it was Disruptive. And spawned a multi-million dollar spin-off industry of merchandise. It isn't often that an advertising idea gives birth to T-shirts, Kewpie dolls and all manner of *tchotchke.*

Simple and effective, right?

Only it wasn't so simple. Because over the course of time the brain trust at Energizer twisted and contorted the idea until, ironically, there was no juice left in it.

(Full disclosure, I was freelancing at Chiat/Day and witnessed the whole draining affair.)

Keep Going was replaced, or nudged aside, with "That's Positivenergy™."

I have no idea what that means. Nor, I believe, do the focus group attendants who will say anything to collect their $75 and eat free tuna fish sandwiches and stale peanut M&M's.

It wasn't the first time a client took the goose that laid the golden eggs and sacrificed it on the altar of mediocrity. Nor the first time an agency, a holding company agency, long-divested of a spine, responded by saying...

"Sure, Mr. or Ms. New CMO, we can do that. Here's the invoice for April."

Just recently, the agency handling the Dos Equis account retired the Most Interesting Man in the World. I suspect some Big Data mining executives and Digital Content Strategy Innovators came to the conclusion that people who drink beer want to see a younger, hipper spokesperson. Maybe a guy with a lumberjack beard, who can dance.

They literally took the best asset the brand had and put it

on a one way death rocket to Mars.

We have yet to see what they will do to replace the Most Interesting Man in the World.

But I'm going to go out on a limb and predict it will be a lot less interesting.

12 Years a Slave-Free Freelancer

Facebook sent me a reminder last week.

Linkedin.com sent me the same reminder today.

And my wife, in her own passive/aggressive manner, echoed the same sentiments recently when she said...

"It's been 12 years now, when are you going to get a real job?"

Well, I'm only 44 years old and it may be a bit premature to make any conjectures, but I'm pretty sure the job I have now, as a free-roaming, creative mercenary, will be the job that I have until the day I retire.

That is unless WPP takes me up on my suggestion, replaces Sir Martin Sorrell and names me the new Chairman.

How shortsighted of them not to even fly me out (business class) to NYC, put me up at a swanky old man hotel, not one of the Eurotrash boutiques with the waterfall urinals, take me to a nice steakhouse, the kind where old Mafia captains would get shot, and hear out my proposals for righting the ship that seems eager to find its resting place at the bottom of the Marianna Trench.

But it's exactly that type of corporate myopia that has kept me at arm's length from the agency world.

A short arm to be completely accurate. Because let's face it, the bulk of my business still comes from the ad agencies, who call me and the growing battalions of freelancers, usually at the last minute, and usually with a hint of desperation in their breath:

"The client's not happy with the work they have been dictating to us for the last 18 months and wants to do something different -- a whole new brand direction. Can you come in Monday? And we can only afford you through Wednesday."

And I'm more than happy to oblige.

But, I'm even happier these days to be fielding calls directly from clients.

And this is happening more and more.

Projects from clients who see my age and my experience as an asset. Clients who are more than happy to save vital office space and want me to work remotely. Clients who trust in the process and do not require mid day, mid evening and mid morning check ins. Clients who actually want to hear my Lee Clow/Chiat/Day war stories.

There's a tidal wave of change coming to the business.

And maybe it's the flurry of recent bank deposits talking, but I think the next twelve years are going to be better than the first.

Now Trending…

As I've mentioned before, I like to stay abreast on all industry news. I like to know where clients are going. Where employees are going. And where trends are going.

It's part and parcel of being a copywriter. I like to think I'm a good observer of human behavior.

It's how, for instance, I know that people don't want to give up the steering wheel for a driverless car. Or how they will never be convinced to eat pizza backwards. Or how, despite the tommyrot dished out by management about greater collaboration and increased productivity, people do not want to work in an open office plan.

They just don't.

Lately, I've noticed a very troubling trend in the ad industry.

OK, there are many troubling trends in the ad industry, but this one is gaining steam.

Perhaps you've noticed it too.

An agency will hire a bevy of heavy hitting C-Suite executives. They have fancy titles. Impressive resumes. And they come furnished with their own professionally shot, heavily photoshopped 8 X 10 headshots. Any agency would be proud to have these tattooed wonders on board. Digital is their native language. And clients can't get enough of their paradigm-changing bullcockery.

So says the press releases on AgencySpy

Then, a week, maybe two weeks later, that same agency – and there are many I've seen doing this – will "downsize" or "rightsize" or "trim the fat" and lay off a bevy of not-so-heavy-hitting staffers.

People who actually do the work. You know, the peons who gave up their nights and weekends and missed birthday parties for mismanaged new business pitches or last minute brand turnarounds.

Those folks.

It doesn't take a genius to spot this trend. The fact that I noticed it, is proof of that. But it certainly is indicative of the level of tone deafness that is increasing on a daily basis.

There used to be a joke, *"don't let the door hit you in the ass on the way out."*

Now it's, *"Don't let the door hit you on the way out and could you please hold it open for our new Chief Innovations Platform Anthropologist?"*

Honey Badger Do Care

In my early days as a staff copywriter I was told – on many occasions – that I cared too much.

I was raised to believe that if I was going to do a job I might as well do it right. So caring too much never made any sense. There were other cliches as well. All equally baffling.

"You need to learn to pick your battles."

"Don't fall on your sword so often."

"I think your works sucks, but don't take it personally."

As I've mentioned before, that led to a great many heated confrontations. Rightly or wrongly, in hindsight mostly wrongly, I took great pride in my work and what I put on the table.

Eventually the hairs on my head stopped growing. The hair in my ears started growing. And my skin got thicker. Meaning I became more immune to the slings and arrows aimed squarely at my ideas.

I'm 44 now.
No longer a staffer, but a sniper.
Just a paid mercenary to come in, take the shot, and collect a check.

The wisdom that was wasted on my youth is finally sinking in. I think I've finally kicked this annoying caring habit.

Well, almost.

Last week I was hired to do a job, remotely. I was dealing directly with the Chief Creative Officer, who was looking for platforms, TV scripts and digital engagement ideas. In other words, my perfect working conditions.

At the end of each day, I would send my progress to the remote location. And at the beginning of the next day I would receive feedback. This is where it gets tricky, because it's hard not to care when the reactions goes something like this (not to violate any NDA's but these are verbatim):

"Great stuff."

"LOL, Love you, Rich."

"Awesome."

"FUUUUKKKKKK, these are perfect."

Each of these appreciative quips were followed by a detailed lengthy directive on what was expected next. Orderly, concise, and to the point because it came directly from the top. For one brief week I actually enjoyed what I was doing and had some fun at this advertising business.

I hope that's not going to be a problem.

Razor Sharp Wit.

The great thing about the universe is how it strives for balance.

Unseen, unknown forces are hard at work to provide a ying for every yang. A dog for every cat. A new calorie-burning cardio machine for every slice of German Triple Chocolate Forest Cake.

This great movement towards self-balance is also evident in the world of business.

Take Theranos for example. At one time this Silicon Valley wundercompany was valued at more than $9 billion. Today, the maker of medical diagnostic toys that literally wanted your blood, is worth less than the bandaids needed to cover up the pricks.

The ying to this particular yang is the Dollar Shave Club. A start up that had zero valuation in its infancy was just sold to Unilever for $1 billion.

And that's not faux Wall Street wall paper money, that's one billion dollars in greenbacks -- the kind of real cash you can use to buy groceries, purchase dry cleaning services or even hand over to your personal physician for verifiable medical testing.

Clearly I am delighted with the success of Dollar Shave Club.

Why? Because it can be argued the company owes its unprecedented success to marketing.

Truth is, monthly purchasing clubs have been with us for a while. You can have fruits and cheese delivered to your doorstep. You can have tailored shirts delivered to your doorstep. You can even join a purchasing outfit that will send you a new golf club every month.

Razor blades are just the latest commodity to join the list. What stood out was the way those shaving utensils were brought to market.

Perhaps you're familiar with their quirky, breakthrough videos. If not, you'd be wise to visit YouTube and see for yourself. Of course my joy for Dollar Shave Club is tinged with some bitterness. It's like digging into a delicious chopped salad only to discover the chef has misguidedly added in some turnips.

Or beets.

You see I've spent the entirety of my career pitching ideas of a similar nature.

Deadpan delivery. Intelligent copy. A nod to the absurd. And for the entirety of my career I have returned from those pitch meetings hearing the same tired responses:

"We like humor, but we're not looking for laughs."

How silly of me.

It may not have worked out in my case, but congratulations Dollar Shaving Club. You have proven that old maxim...

Funny is Money.

Calculus 101

When I tell people I used to work at Chiat/Day they always want to know what it was like to present work to Lee Clow. They presume the experience to be intimidating and nerve-wracking. And to some extent, it was.

But I always found that was more self-induced.

When it came to judging work and whether that work had any merit to move forward, Lee was always surprisingly brief.

"Yes." "No." "No." "Yes." "No." "No."
"Definitely No."

(OK, I'm being generous, there was one Yes for every 20 No's.)

The work that passed the yes/no test was always followed with, "That could be funny", "That could be cool", "That could be interesting." Meaning, this has promise, but a lot more work had to be done.

What I find interesting is how the judging criteria has changed over the years.

You see, I rarely hear those type of phrases anymore. Today, work gets held up to a different measuring stick: the check list.

"This spot has plenty of innovation, but not enough humanity."

"This talks about our features, but not enough about the benefits."

"This speaks about our heritage, but not enough about our future."

If you work in the Creative Department of an ad agency you know exactly what I'm talking about. A brief may have one single communications message, but a good planner knows how to utilize every inch of white space on a page. So that one overriding message will be buttressed with five or six under-riding messages.

These requests can be cleverly disguised as Tone, Copy Support, or the very threatening, Mandatories.

And just because they're at the bottom of the page doesn't make them any less important. They're all important.

In the end, a spot that was designed to convey X, must also include mentions of Y and Z, while at the same time implying *leadership, innovation, customer service and dependability.*

When it's all said and done, the brief looks less like a strategy for success and more like a recipe for something you would never want to eat.

Please bake a cake with the following ingredients:

2 lbs. white flour
1/2 lbs. ground beef
4 ounces of milk chocolate

3 tablespoons of cayenne pepper
3 ounces 10W-40 motor oil
8 stalks of celery
A dash of curry
A sprinkling of saffron
A smidgeon of Kosher Salt
A pinch of Plutonium

And we need it by 4 PM.

Our Day with Ally Sheedy

The 1970's are considered to be the height of American cinema. That storied decade gave us *The Godfather, The French Connection, One Flew Over the Cuckoo's Nest, Dog Day Afternoon,* and *Manhattan.*

Sadly, the 1980's followed with such stellar films as *Yentl, Ishtar,* and *Over The Top.*

1985 also gave us the *Breakfast Club,* a breakout vehicle for many brat packers including Judd Nelson, Emilio Estevez and Anthony Michael Hall – all of whom went on to make a huge impact and forever change the face of the thespianic arts.

I know that for many *Breakfast Club* has a lot of nostalgic value. For me it has none. Well, almost none.

You see following its release, another star, Ally Sheedy, also found instant fame and was quickly catapulted onto the A-list of actresses. Determined not to become a rom-com princess in the John Hughes fantasy world, Ally began searching out meatier, more dramatic roles. And she became a Method Actor.

So when she agreed to play the character of a fast rising art director at a hip ad agency there was only one thing to do – hang out with a fast-rising creative team at Chiat/Day.

Perhaps because all the other teams were involved with

some award-winning campaigns, and because we were not, we were chosen for the task.

The plan was for Ms. Sheedy to spend an entire day with my partner and I to get a feel for what we did and how we did it.

If memory serves, she strolled in around 11 o'clock. We exchanged some small talk. She was very pleasant. And then she watched as my partner kerned some body copy and asked me to fill in some widows on a 1/2 page ad for the 1993 Nissan Maxima.

Hardly the stuff of Shakespeare.

She took us to lunch at the Rose Cafe and returned to the office so she could watch us get briefed on a new assignment and shoot rubber bands at the other creative teams in the adjoining cubicles.

In addition to her high cheekbones and strong chin, it became evident that Ms. Sheedy had also been blessed with a quick mind.

Because by 2:30 PM her limo showed up and she was out of there.

We eagerly awaited the movie's release. Hoping to get a screen credit as technical consultants. But like so many Hollywood dreams, we were crushed. We found out the film got shitcanned.

Apparently the studio execs came to the conclusion that movies about people in advertising are just not that interesting.

I could have saved them millions of development dollars. I have 4 half-written screenplays to that effect.

Bone Us.

The Christmas Bonus.

It's that time of year again, when none of us will get one.

Of course that wasn't always the case. I remember getting my first Xmas bonus. It was my first year in the corporate world. There I was, a lowly mailroom clerk, seated among some of the most highly regarded creative professionals in the ad industry. People responsible for making Los Angeles a legitimate advertising town.

We were at the Riviera Country Club, where, ironically enough, I would return 10 years later to get married.

Agency Principal Gerry Rubin, decked out in a fancy suit and an even fancier cowboy hat, strutted around the banquet room handing out envelopes. He approached me, shook my hand, thanked me for all the hard work I had put in that year, though I'm absolutely sure he did not even know my name.

Nevertheless, he placed a #10 Navajo White envelope on my place setting.

The more seasoned folks simply placed the envelope in their coat pocket or their purse. I had none of that well-practiced Protestant restraint. I ripped it open before Gerry had moved on to the next table. Inside, I found (1) incredibly-crisp, never-been-folded hundred dollar bill.

Until that point in my life, I'd never held an actual C-note.
I was giddy with excitement. And thought, naively I might
add, this is just the beginning. This is going to get better
and bigger with every passing year in the ad business.

It did not.

Apparently Southern California ad agencies – and I've
worked at all of them – have been in a recession and in
frugality mode for the last 30 consecutive years. Monetary
bonuses were soon replaced with baubles. Umbrellas.
Hoodies. Moleskin writing tablets. When that got too
costly, agencies went to gestures.

*"In lieu of a gift we have generously made a donation to the
Don't Eat the Dolphins Fund in your name."*

Never acknowledging that this charitable donation made
for a healthy year tax write-off.

For the agency that is.

And soon the gestures became distant memories. Not only
had the Christmas bonus vanished, the grumbling about
not getting a year end or Xmas bonus had also disappeared.
Today savvy staffers, who are lucky that they have a job,
know to keep their mouths shut.

After all, happy shareholders are more important than
happy employees.

I work for a very small company now. In fact, we only have one employee: Rich Siegel.

And he's done a fantastic job this year. So he's going to get a bonus. And an expensive bottle of bourbon. And some new underwear. And we're going to make a donation to Red Cross in his name. And to top it all off, we're even going to let him write the charitable gift off *his* tax return.

Merry Christmas, Rich.

An Apology

Just for giggles, I decided to write out the script for the now-famous Old Spice campaign. I'm not sure this is what the script looked like, I simply transcribed it from a YouTube video.

On paper, it doesn't look like much. There's a lot of copy. A lot of screen action. And frankly, it sounds like there's too much math going on, meaning it's too complicated.

"MAN SMELL"
:30

Open on athletic looking man stepping out of the shower, wearing a towel around his waist.

MAN: **Hello Ladies.**

Camera drifts in on the man.

MAN: **Look at your man, now back to me. Now back to your man, now back to me. Sadly, he isn't me. But if he stopped using lady-scented body wash…**

Man holds up a bottle of Old Spice.

MAN: **He could smell like he is me.**

The shower behind him rises like a curtain and the props of the bathroom are pulled away, leaving the man on a boat.

MAN: **Look down, back up. Where are you?**

A beach shirt tied in a ring drops down and falls around the man's neck.

MAN: **You're on a boat with a man your man could smell like.**

Camera drifts in tighter on man.

MAN: **What's in your hand? Back at me. I have it.**

The man is now holding a large oyster.

MAN: **It's an oyster with two tickets to that thing you love.**

The oyster magically turns into a handful of diamonds.

MAN: **Look again. The tickets are now diamonds.**

A bottle of Old Spice rises from the diamonds.

MAN: **Anything is possible when your man smells like Old Spice and not a lady.**

The camera drifts back and the man is now longer on a

boat, but sitting on a horse.

MAN: **I'm on a horse.**

SUPER: **Smell like a man, man.**

LOGO: **Old Spice.**

Whistle Mnemonic

If a young team brought me this idea when I was a Creative Director, I'm pretty sure I would have sent that team back to the drawing board. I might have said something stupid like, "there's not enough sell in this" or "make it shorter" or even "It doesn't seem funny."

And that's troublesome, because work like this can make or break a career.

I've had a lot of talented people work for me in the past. I am positive that at one time or another I killed a script that could have been great.

And so, today I'm going to do what my family says I never do: apologize.

I am really sorry.

SIEGEL: **I'm on a knee.**

The Write Stuff

Lately, I have been back on the agency circuit, popping in and out of various ad agencies, large and small.

Or in the parlance of prostitutes, I've been 'doing the ho stroll.'

The comparison is not all that labored. After all, I'm willing to pimp out my ideas to any needy agency with a brief in one hand and an oversized check in the other.

And since I've been visiting these various agencies (five if I've counted correctly) I've noticed a tidal wave of change in the Creative Department.

They're all kids!

Mind you, I've always been aware that the Creative Department was getting younger and younger as the hair gathering at the bottom of my shower drain was getting thicker and thicker. And I understand the need to bring in fresh faces who are much more in touch with pop culture than I could ever be. But I always believed that pool of youth needed to be balanced with an equal distribution of seasoned writers and art directors who knew a little something about craft.

Apparently, I was wrong.

With my own daughters away at Jew Camp, I've enjoyed an extra dose of free time. So, being envious of their youth and curious about their credentials, I did a little digging. And I checked out this new confident crop of creatives, who are more than eager to boast about their achievements via social media.

Holy Diaper Change, Batman!

Most of these youngsters, who now call themselves professional writers or art directors, weren't even in the ad business three years ago.

They were folding shirts at The Gap or playing field hockey for their college intra-mural team. Now they're stewarding global brands and bringing their formidable life experience to bear down on complex billion dollar marketing challenges.

It's as if someone in Accounting or HR said, "I like the way that new intern never leaves the coffee pot empty and always brews a fresh batch, let's make him or her a Creative Director."

I know this little rant is inviting a certain predictable response along the lines of, "Shut up old man" or "Shut up very old man". But the truth is, I'm just making an observation, I'm not complaining at all. And I'm not commenting on their work. Because the other truth is, some of them, not all, are actually talented.

But if you were to check the linkedin profiles of these kids, particularly the copywriters, who in effect are my competition, you'd see what I saw: links that don't work, ghastly grammar, and sloppy portfolios and resumes peppered with typos. Did I say peppered? I meant smothered.

You would also see what I didn't: writing.

Nothing in the way of great headlines.

Or long body copy.

Or any evidence of a passion for the written word.

But like I said, I'm not complaining. Because when an agency is staffed by writers who don't write, there is often a time when they need one who does.

Imported from Detroit

You've probably seen this line before.

Clint Eastwood breathed life into it at the Super Bowl, in a Chrysler commercial that made all the headlines. And the folks at Wieden & Kennedy, the ad agency for Chrysler, have been using it for more than a year now. What you don't know is that now-famous tagline, merchandised on T-shirts, coffee mugs, backpacks, etc., almost belonged to Chevrolet, not Chrysler.

Wait. What?

The year was 2009. My art director partner and I were doing work for Publicis in Seattle. They were in the process of courting Chevrolet and pulling the account away from Campbell Ewald.

The effort was all hands on deck. And for a $600 million account one can understand why. There were weekends, late nights and fast, fast turnarounds. But we were all too willing to ride the freelance gravy train.

Those were heady, well-paid days. And Publicis reaped the rewards. They won the account and celebrated accordingly. (Sadly, the victory didn't last long as months later, the account was yanked and handed to GS&P, but that's a different story.)

At one point in the transition, we were asked to do a tagline exploration.

The goal was to rebrand Chevrolet and give people a reason to believe American-built cars were as good as the ones being exported from Germany and Japan.

Well, you guessed it, one of the lines we submitted was: **Chevrolet. Imported from Detroit.**

For reasons that elude me, the creative director rejected the line. I don't hold it against him. When you look at 1000 possible tag lines they often blur together and become meaningless. Maybe he thought the line was a bit of an overpromise. It doesn't matter because a tagline is only as good as the work that surrounds it.

I'm not sure what work we would have done around that particular line. I am sure I never would have arrived at that signature piece of music that is now on every Chrysler commercial. I like the music, it feels gritty and urban and Detroit, and it sure sticks in your head, it's just not in my repertoire. Which tells me I need to expand my repertoire.

In the end this story gets filed under the 100 Monkey Phenomena. (Put 100 monkeys on keyboards and given enough time one of them will eventually type out a Shakespearean play.)

In the U.S. there are about 20-30 different car brands. Those brands are handled by different ad agencies. Each agency has about 10-15 creative people coming with ideas for the brand. Writers and art directors, working night and day, saying the same thing about the same cars, everyday of every week of every month of every year. So, in accordance with the theory obviously there's going to be some duplication.

The way I see it, I'm one of 450 ad monkeys.

I just happened to get snake bit by one of them.

I'm Such a Tool

It's typical for a man my age, 44, to look back on his life and start wondering about some of the choices that have been made or the roads that have been followed.

I've been doing a little bit of soul searching lately and come to the undeniable conclusion that I am a Grade A Douchebag.

Particularly when it comes to the particulars of my career.

For years, I thought the proper – the only – way to go about making a TV commercial for our high paying clients was to dig into their business, understand their position in the marketplace, rethink their approach and then create and devise a strategic piece of communication that would alter their public perception and drive consumers to their products or services.

What was I smoking?

When I watch a commercial today it becomes painfully obvious that I wasted so much time and energy trying to bring some silly high-minded concept to the small screen.

I can feel my kidneys clench when I mull over all those scripts, all those hours, all those heated discussions with planners, account people and clients, just trying to will my way to something worthwhile.

Now, in retrospect, it's all clear to me, 'ideas' are so 1990's.

If I were a junior copywriter coming up through the ranks today, I'd do it all different. I'd put down the acrimony and pick up The Formula. Oh you know The Formula. It may not have been formally committed to paper, but it is the How-To Manual for almost everything that shows up on TV today.

1. Get a Top Ten Song. Thanks to the advent of iTunes, these are easy to find. No need for expensive scoring or laborious searches for just the right soundtrack. Pick a song people know, preferably sung or arranged by an alternative indie band. Ideally, a photogenic alternative indie band. When in doubt, look for beanie caps, full sleeve tats and Amish/lumberjack beards. This way you'll have some youthful eye candy for the obligatory behind-the-scenes making of the commercial video that people flock to on YouTube.

2. Hire yourself a B list director. These are typically former A list directors who have grown accustomed to a certain lifestyle. Now, no longer in feverish demand, they have dropped a rung or two on the ladder but still enjoy hob-knobbing in Cannes. To do so, they will do what they do, with much less opinionating and much more accommodating. Oh and they're a lot cheaper.

3. The Abercrombie & Fitch approach to casting. It goes without saying that every spot should be a Rainbow Coalition of people. Three white males must always be

accompanied by an African American. And two white
females must always have a sassy sister. And all of them
must be pretty damn hot or cute, preferably both. No one
wants to see ugly people. Ugly people shop at Walmart. So
you must cast impossibly attractive actors. Even if you're
shooting a spot for Walmart.

4. Change the world, at least pretend to. In case you
hadn't noticed people like companies that like people.
Companies that want to enrich our planet while enriching
their bank accounts. Anybody can sell drain cleaners or
paper towels or melted cheese in a squeezable bottle,
but the buying public wants to conduct commerce with
companies who care. Being attached to a cause is the cost
of doing business these days. That applies to everyone,
including manufacturers of pourable cheddar-like
substances.

**5. Say everything but say nothing. Or Platitudes not
Attitudes.** Planners know exactly what it is consumers
want to see and hear. That's why they're planners. You'd
be silly to ignore their supernatural wisdom and uncanny
understanding of all the complexities of human behavior.
Study their ways. Learn their language. Mirror their every
move. And soon you too will know the difference between
an Innovative Challenger and a Motivated Influencer.
Gold lions, gold pencils and gold Telly awards will be
yours for the asking.

There you have it. I've done everything but regurgitate the brief...uhhhh, write the script for you.

Which I'll be happy to do in 2017 with the new adjusted-for-inflation-and-my-daughter's-college-tuition 2017 Day Rates.

Did I mention that a portion of every day rate earned will be donated to the St. Jude's Research Hospital?

One postscript - don't forget those hashtags.

II

About the Author

At this point, in many books, the author goes on to brag about past achievements: prior books he or she has published, perhaps an article reprinted in the New Yorker or The Atlantic, or even something more mundane, like putting in a respectable time in the local 10K race.

I'm not going to do any of that. I'm thinking by now you're probably sick of hearing me talking about me. I know I am.

Instead, I'd like to acknowledge some people who may or may not have contributed to this book but would nevertheless love to see their name in print.

For helping with the cover, formatting and interior design, thanks go out to Robert Prins and Bonnie Miguel.

For respecting and abiding by the laws governing the Man Cave, and allowing me time to write, thanks to my wife Debra and my two lovely daughters, Rachel and Abby.

And for carelessly nosediving the entire advertising industry into the ground, and in doing so, inspiring many, many stories, my eternal thanks to the four holding companies and their esteemed sagacious leadership.

57182418R00168

Made in the USA
Lexington, KY
08 November 2016